MARK RUTLAND

Word of Life Series

POWER discover
personal strength
in one word

Charisma
HOUSE
A STRANG COMPANY

Most STRANG COMMUNICATIONS/CHARISMA HOUSE/SILOAM products are available at special quantity discounts for bulk purchase for sales promotions, premiums, fund-raising, and educational needs. For details, write Strang Communications/Charisma House/Siloam, 600 Rinehart Road, Lake Mary, Florida 32746, or telephone (407) 333-0600.

POWER by Mark Rutland
Published by Charisma House
A Strang Company
600 Rinehart Road
Lake Mary, Florida 32746
www.charismahouse.com

Unless otherwise noted, all Scripture quotations are from the King James Version of the Bible.

Cover design by Rachel Campbell

Library of Congress Cataloging-in-Publication Data

Rutland, Mark.
   Power/Mark Rutland.
      p.cm
   ISBN 1-59185-277-3 (hardback)
   1. God--Omnipotence. 2. Power--Religious aspects--
   Christianity. l.
   Title. BT133.R88 2004
   261.8--dc22

                                        2003021233
04 05 06 07 08 — 987654321
Printed in the United States of America

To Alison
Did you know that you're my hero?

ACKNOWLEDGMENTS

My deepest gratitude is to my wife, Alison, whose intellect and professionalism continue to challenge me, whose faith inspires me, and whose grace amazes me. She, without whom I would be nothing, has always been willing to wait, to watch while the light shone over me; yet she seeks so little for herself. Much of what I have learned and written about the attitudes of Christ I have seen and been blessed by in her.

The manuscript did not prepare itself. Page after page, book after book, Mrs. Glenna Rakes and Dr. Gordon Miller managed somehow to translate my hieroglyphics.

Finally, my thanks go to Stephen Strang, Barbara Dycus, and all the others at Strang Communications and Charisma House. I am grateful for the partnership. May God grant you power to live and to serve and to glorify Him.

CONTENTS

PART I

Power, Not Power

Those who have been once intoxicated with power, and have derived any kind of emolument from it, even though but for one year, never can willingly abandon it. They may be distressed in the midst of all their power; but they will never look to anything but power for their relief.

—EDMUND BURKE

THE PROMISE OF POWER

One night in a cave near Caesarea Philippi, Jesus peered across the campfire and stunned His disciples by asking aloud the question they had hardly dared whisper to each other in private:

"Whom do men say that I am?"

The question, staggering in its implications, hung suspended in the air and sucked all the oxygen out of the cave. Like guppies pitched up onto the bank, the disciples limply murmured the popular answers, such as John the Baptist and Elijah. They searched the Master's face for a clue, some response, perhaps a word of affirmation to reveal that, yes, that's the correct answer.

Jesus ignored their answers, choosing instead to turn the question onto the disciples: "Whom say ye that I am?"

Frozen in fear and confusion they gaped at the Master. The wrong answer could mean death or, at the very least, horrifying embarrassment, and none knew the right answer anyway. Elijah? If not Elijah, who? Rabbi? Judge? Deliverer? Exorcist? Man of miracles? No answer, right or wrong, dared leap to their lips. Silence thick and terrible filled the cave, and not a word was spoken.

"You are the Christ." Peter, always Peter, bold and

fearless to a fault, ruptured the quiet with a raspy whisper that sounded, in the silence, like a roar. "You are the Son of the living God."

A gasp, and instantly every eye was on Jesus. Would He rebuke Peter, perhaps with a slap on the mouth, the ancient Jewish response to blasphemy? Indeed, if Peter was wrong he deserved to be slapped or even stoned. To identify a natural man as the Son of God is the most horrifying heresy imaginable. Furthermore, there was no way for Peter to be kind of... almost... nearly... sort of right—not when he used such bold language. "You are the Son of the living God." That statement is either 100 percent right or 100 percent wrong.

Jesus' answer, however, left no room for doubt. "You are right," Jesus said, then added, "You have not heard this from any human, but from God." The others were astonished. There it was. The answer to all their questions was now in the open. Jesus was not a mere prophet or an unusually anointed rabbi, but Messiah Immanuel, the Son of the living God.

The disciples were ablaze with excitement and anticipation. The announcement of His Sonship having been made officially, Jesus set His face toward Jerusalem and, best of all, invited the disciples to go with Him and to share in all that lay ahead. Obviously He was going there to claim David's throne and to be the *new* David, to reestablish the Davidic dynasty and rule the kingdom from its historic capital, Jerusalem. They were in on the ground floor. They were going to share in whatever kingdom, glory, and power were coming.

Now, He said, as if he heard their thoughts, "Let's go to Jerusalem." *Jerusalem!* No new kingdom of Israel could be ruled from Galilee or from anywhere except Jerusalem. This was it! The historic moment was upon them. Jesus was going to Jerusalem to seize power, and they would be His eager underlords. As they journeyed toward Jerusalem, they were mentally dividing up the kingdoms of the earth, fantasizing about which apostle would rule which province.

They understood their power was subject to His. They were to be the twelve kings of the earth and He the King of kings. They were happy to play Ptolemy to His Alexander, letting Him rule over them while they ruled over everyone else. Ultimate power was not their fantasy. A share, twelve equal shares, was fantasy enough for a gaggle of common fishers such as they.

Jesus would get the main throne. They all knew that. The twelve smaller thrones, six on each side of His, were their concern. Only the mother of James and John was bold enough to petition for any particular position. She reasoned that the chairs on either side of the central throne would be the seats of greatest power, and she requested them for her sons. Mrs. Zebedee knew that the twelve would be equal.

She did not contest that. She just wanted her boys to be a little more equal. After all, if power was to be shared, let her sons be the closest to the throne.

Jesus' triumphal return to Jerusalem did nothing but reinforce this paradigm. As His tiny entourage wound its way down the Mount of Olives toward Kidron and the Temple mound, the populace seemed to sense what the apostles now knew. Jesus was entering the city to establish His kingdom and rule the new Israel from His throne in Jerusalem.

"Hosanna!" the throng shouted. "Save us now!"

The Master was about to become the king. It was in the air. The crowds sensed it. So did the apostles, and they were delirious. They had been powerless far too long, ground under the boots of Gentile domination, and they were ready for power to be theirs for a change.

From the parapets of the Antonia Fortress next to the temple, Roman soldiers studied the tumult suspiciously. Let them watch! Let them hear the shouts of the crowd. Let them see the waving palms and dancing, happy Jews receiving and rejoicing in their king. Soon Jerusalem, not Rome, would wield the power. Old scores would be settled as the tables were turned the other way. Let them watch. The king was entering his city in triumph.

The Pharisees also watched and knew the Romans saw it all. Busy as old women, their skirts flapping anxiously, the Pharisees swarmed to protect the city from its king.

"Make them be quiet," they fussed.

"The Romans will see."

"We will all be killed."

"Master, they are calling You a king. Silence them for all our sakes."

Jesus' answer dumbfounded them all.

"If these should be silent, the stones will cry out."

"What?" They gaped. They stared at Him, at each other, at the sky. What could that possibly mean?

It didn't matter to the broiling throng that lined the roadway. They had hardly understood a word Jesus had said in three years. It sounded good, must be good, must be wonderful. Yes, let the rocks join the celebration.

The joyous knot of wildly happy humanity jostled and tumbled down the winding road. Then it snaked upward from the Kidron Valley toward the temple mound. Behind the throng the Pharisees watched in envious hatred and fearful apprehension. Above them, in the towers of the fortress named for Marc Anthony, Roman soldiers watched in condescension and disdain, no more concerned than if the mob had been ants. Indeed, ants or Jews, if they got out of hand, the sole of a Roman boot would squash them just the same.

The apostles were on fire with anticipation. This was what their fathers had waited on, had prayed for in Babylon and Egypt, had longed for in Persia, and been promised by the prophets. Jesus was on the verge of seizing power, power to be shared with them. As Jesus started up the Huldah steps, their hearts thundered within their breasts. If He wanted to claim a new kingdom for Israel, the temple was the only place to announce it.

And announce He did. Up the Huldah steps, through the underground passage, and out into the Court of Gentiles, the raucous crowd followed Jesus right onto the temple mound. They watched as He silently braided three strands of rope into a thick whip, then stood by in shock as He hurled Himself upon the moneychangers at their desks along Solomon's portico. Fury in His eyes, rage unmasked on His face, Jesus charged among them, kicking over their tables and lashing them like an irate livestock manager in a pen of wild donkeys. His voice, a thunderstorm crashing over their heads, was even more terrifying than the rude, knotty whip.

"This is My Father's house. You have dared to make it a den of thieves."

His exact words, even more than the wild, angry thrashing He gave the moneychangers, shot like lightning through the crowd and the disciples. "My Father's house…" Not *the* Father. Not *our* Father. He said, "*My* Father's house." Those words left no doubt. He was the first since David to call God "My Father."

The new David, whip in hand like a scepter, had claimed first the city and now the temple.

The multitude was ecstatic, the disciples delirious, and the Pharisees enraged and utterly unimpressed. They knew a cheap demagogue when they saw one. Such self-anointed messiahs mad with lust for personal power did not fool them. They exchanged knowing glances. They had seen His kind before. Self-righteous, sent from God, full of secret revelations known only to themselves, these messiahs caused confusion, created uproar, and unfailingly got someone—usually themselves—killed.

John the Baptist had shaken the nation, but he died like a fool in Herod's prison. The Sanhedrin wasted no time mourning his loss. Now this Galilean had come. Subtler, smarter, and infinitely more dangerous than the Baptist, this Jesus, like John, like all such prophetic types, had no idea how lethal an incendiary He really was. His bold grab for power was doomed, of that they were certain. The question was how many others would die before they were at last rid of Him.

The Sanhedrin mocked the carefully orchestrated "spontaneous" demonstration in the streets. Jesus' followers had whipped the people into a lather, and Jesus had whipped the moneychangers into retreat. Well, he who wields a whip can be made to feel it, and mobs can be manipulated one way as well as another.

Jesus loved to make His milky little speeches about forgiveness and faith and the lilies of the field, but with the sweat of wrath upon His brow and the lash in His hand, He was the real hypocrite. If He wanted to play power games He should have stayed in Nazareth. In Jerusalem He was over His head—here the Sanhedrin wielded the real power. Not even Rome, especially not that arrogant swine of a governor, had any real power. Oh, the Romans could kill excellently. They were, in fact, useful for that. Real power, however, means to control the outcome, and in Jerusalem, all the important outcomes were determined by the Sanhedrin. Pilate could be manipulated to do what they wanted because they knew how to pull his strings. Herod was able to kill— indeed, he had killed John the Baptist in his drunken lust—but the Sanhedrin had already decided his fate. Herod was simply their fool of an executioner. Now this Jesus matter had been decided as well. It was as settled as if it had already been done. Today He had put out His hand for power. He should have stayed in Galilee working miracles. The power He grabbed for on this day would be His undoing.

By sundown the disciples were exhausted. When at last the day's excitement was gone, they returned to Gethsemane for a light supper, and dusk under the olive trees proved an irresistible soporific. Their minds, fatigued by a day of historic proportions, needed little inducement to sleep. They saw Him praying, if what He did there could be called prayer. Why such apparent struggle? They would never understand Him. Today the people had been ready to crown Him king; the authorities stood by and let Him lay claim to the holy temple, and yet tonight He agonized as though He had just lost a terrible war. Let Him pray. He prayed too much. It couldn't be healthy to pray that much. Tonight they needed sleep, not prayer. Despite Jesus' summons to prayer, in moments their unconscious forms littered the garden floor.

When the soldiers came, they were still sleeping. Confusion banished peace from the quiet garden, and suddenly all was torches, shouts, and clanging armor. No one knew what to do. Peter, as usual, did the wrong thing, slashing off one guard's ear with a sword. Jesus rebuked Peter's response and restored the guard's ear. In minutes it was over. The band of soldiers, their prize in tow, wound back through the silent streets. An ominous dread engulfed the disciples.

Within hours it was all finished. Not only the body of Jesus but also their dreams of power were crucified, dead, and buried. Entombed with Him behind a massive stone lay all their messianic dreams of power in the new kingdom of a new David. Finished. Nothing. Where once their visions of grandeur stood, despair now lay like the ruins of a conquered city.

Then came the women, Mary Magdalene in

particular, claiming to have seen Him alive again. What should they make of that? Next, Judas's rumored suicide was confirmed. Would all this never end? Even in death Jesus seemed able to keep their lives in constant confusion. Still others came with reports of Jesus' appearances in Jerusalem and Emmaus.

In hushed conspiratorial tones behind closed doors, they gathered the ragged reports into a single bundle and tried to make some sense of it all. It was useless. Theories met countertheories, hopes and brave words of faith ran up against sullen doubt, and no consensus could be found. Thomas, not usually given to speeches or strong opinions, finally framed the discussion for them all.

"Look," he said, "I cannot live this way anymore. While He lived, we wondered who He was. Now that He is dead, we wonder if He is alive. I can't live at this level of confusion anymore, ever again. For three years we hoped that He would announce Himself as king. When He did, He was killed. Now that He is *dead—dead*, do you hear me?—we want Him to announce Himself as messiah. Well, let Him do so. No more hints. No more guessing games. Power, power, power. It's all we talked about for three years. If He has power over death, that's all the power I need to see. But I have to see it. See it and touch it. If He is alive, *if*, I say, then let me touch the wounds. We all saw Him pierced with nails in His hands. We watched that soldier stab Him in the side. If He is alive, let me touch the wounds. Let me touch the wounds!"

The others stared at Thomas, astonished at this rare display of emotion. Voice raised, nostrils flaring, he brought his palm down on the table in a loud slap. Then softening under their gaze, he added, not in a loud demand, but in a pleading whisper, "I want to believe…as much as any of you. I just can't do this anymore. Let me touch Him, and I will believe."

Suddenly the room flooded with light. The air took on that strange, crackly feeling that it exhibits just before a terrible lightning storm. Then He *was* there.

The power in the room was overwhelming. Nothing else mattered—not Judas, not the past, not their weakness—absolutely nothing else in the universe meant anything. He was alive. What power! What life! It filled the room and saturated the air, making their skin tingle and their spirits dance within them. Alive! Back from the dead.

Day after day, for forty days to be precise, they tried to listen, tried to concentrate, labored to understand what He was saying to them. The problem was Him, the very fact of Him there alive in their presence. They could hardly listen to Him for looking at Him. Gradually and, oh, so incompletely, the message He preached began to penetrate. Finally they understood. That message was the kingdom of God. How often He had taught them in parable after parable. The kingdom is like unto a man with a field, a merchantman seeking pearls, or an old woman searching for a lost coin.

The kingdom that they had expected on that great day of His triumphal entry into Jerusalem, that new kingdom of Israel, was finally to be theirs. Indeed, with Judas gone, each share would be greater. Eleven chairs, not twelve, meant more for everyone. The more Jesus talked about the kingdom, the happier they got. Now they would nail the Romans to the wall, sweep the Sanhedrin away, and execute Herod, that Idumean pretender, just as he had executed John the Baptist. With their leader unbeatable, unkillable, more powerful than death, and greater than Rome, they could not lose.

Finally they could contain themselves no longer. "Now, Lord," they asked Him, their eyes bright with feverish hope, "now will You restore the kingdom to Israel? Now will You sit on the throne in Jerusalem as David did and rule the nations with a rod of iron? Now, Lord?"

Jesus slowly shook His head, a trace of sadness in His eyes. "No, My children. Leave such times and seasons of power in God's hands. You are still seeking power. You shall receive no such power. If you wait for it, you will be disappointed, and you will miss the kingdom. You shall not be given power. But you shall receive power when the Holy Spirit comes upon you. Remember," He said sternly, "you shall receive *power*, not power."

They stared at Him. Again, yet again, just as they had for three years, they marveled. What could He conceivably mean? A kingdom, but not a kingdom? *Power*, not power? They studied their hands, avoiding His eyes and each other's, and prayed for understanding. *Power*, not power? Help us, O Lord.

HAND GRENADES AND HALLELUJAHS

In a seminary in Peru I saw a terrifying poster. A nun in a traditional habit wore a bandoleer of bullets from which dangled several hand grenades. In a holster on her hip was a massive .44 Magnum. With one arm she cradled an Uzi and in the other gripped a 9mm automatic. Underneath, in Spanish, the words said, "A new theology for a new world."

It is not a new theology, of course. The words are couched in terms of the popular Latin heresy of Marxist liberation theology, but the lie is as old as Adam. If God will not give us power, we will seize it. If He will not redeem institutions with His power, we will do it with ours.

There is no difference between a Marxist guerrilla with a Molotov cocktail in her hand and a church rebel with a phone in hers. Refusing to wait on God and denying His sovereignty—both act to rally the troops, foment rebellion, oust authority, and seize control. A nun with a hand grenade and a church member rounding up votes and spreading gossip to remove the pastor are Siamese twins sharing a twisted soul. Both use religious terminology to cover their grab for control. Both believe themselves to be right. Both are demonically dangerous. Both are witches, and neither of them knows it. Hallelujahs and hand grenades are a witch's brew.

After the Resurrection Jesus promised His followers power. He also promised them peace. In the temporal domain, in the realm ruled by time, the followers of Jesus have had precious little of peace or power. The reason, of course, is that Jesus was speaking of an entirely different kind of peace and power.

> Peace I leave with you, my peace I give
> unto you: not as the world giveth, give
> I unto you.
> —JOHN 14:27

In other words, "I give you *peace*, not the world's peace, which is merely the absence of war, but peace beyond time, space, and circumstance." Then, in Acts 1:8, He promised them *power*. For the rest of their lives, those to whom He spoke lived in a maelstrom and were finally put to death by the temporal power systems of politics and religion, the same forces that killed Jesus.

The secret key to spiritual power is understanding

that Jesus means *His* power, different, infinitely more wonderful, majestically more enduring, and ultimately untouched by time. Live and rule in the temporal realm alone, and your power is in time alone, controlled by time, and ended by time. Kings, executives, and bishops who are content with temporal power will never know His, which is beyond all reach of time.

In the movie *True Confession*, Robert De Niro portrays a monsignor corrupted by the games of political intrigue and the constant flow of money around him. An elderly parish priest says to him, "You like power. You like to use it."

"Yes," the monsignor replies. "But how can we do things without it?"

That, in a nutshell, is the question lurking behind the mystery of power. The answer, however, is not, as many think, in how much power we can tolerate. The ancient axiom that power corrupts and absolute power corrupts absolutely is absolutely wrong. The issue is not how much power, but what kind.

Temporal power is power "in time," defined by, limited by, and operating within time. It is for temporal power that the world plots and schemes and does murder. Men lust for power "now," not in a dimension outside of time. Even spiritual power is often desired for what the eternal can do for us in the now. In other words, some may seek spiritual power in ministry for the sake of temporal gain. The power of the eternal, timeless power, made a slave of the temporal, will be corrupted absolutely. There is no evil demonstration of power in the secular world that can begin to compare with the church at its worst. Ecclesiological power brokers who control the lives of churches and the destinies of ministers are in the most vulnerable position.

Those church leaders who conspired to cover up for pedophiles are the obvious example. In what power did they move? Their wheeling and dealing, their withholding evidence and obstructing justice, and their blatant disregard for children was temporal power wielded corruptly in the name of the spiritual.

Other examples, tragic ones, abound. In our twenties, babies in age and in the things of the Spirit, my wife and I saw a miracle faked by some henchmen (I dare to call them that) of a famous minister. It was so blatant, so "in our faces" that ignoring it was not possible. My young wife was hysterical, and I was shaken. We had witnessed a deception, devastating for the poor handicapped man upon whom it was perpetrated and dumbfounding to two naïve kids who were desperate for the authentic things of God.

Weeping and wounded, we knelt and made a covenant with God and each other never to fake an experience, claim a "word" we didn't have, or revise a story to make it more "spiritual." Our prayer was this:

"Lord, we know You are a God of miracles, but our faith does not rest on them. We trust in the God of miracles, not the miracles of God. If we never see another sign, if no wonder ever comes, if no gift is ever manifested, You are I AM. What we will never, ever do is take matters in our hands."

I am terrified that the insinuation of flesh into the activity of the Spirit is rebellion—self-serving, self-glorifying rebellion against the sovereignty of God. Evangelists who emotionally manipulate and physically manhandle seekers are putting themselves and their listeners at risk. Some will say they are "generating faith." God is perfectly capable of generating faith, all the faith that is needed, without the help of embroidered stories and manipulative techniques.

It was less than a year after that disillusioning experience with a false miracle, when, as Forrest Gump put it, "God showed up." I was asked to speak at a large healing conference, large and exciting to a very young man at the beginning of his ministry. At that time I was suffering from the occasional flare-ups of a plantar wart in my left heel. These flare-ups were unbelievably painful.

Of course, that very morning, my own foot chose to betray me. I limped, literally limped onto the platform. Clutching the pulpit for support, I spoke on the healing power of God. Today I have plenty of latitude in my theology for wounded healers, but at twenty-nine I found it unbearably embarrassing to tell others of the healing power of God while I, myself, was in such obvious pain. Now after thirty-five years in ministry, I understand that is what every sermon preached by any pastor anywhere is all about. We are all wounded healers in one way or another.

By the second day of the conference my foot was throbbing. I could not even bear to put on my shoe. Before the service the second night, I lay alone in the darkened auditorium with my foot elevated on the front pew. I was wallowing in self-pity, distracted by the pain, and certain that I would never again be asked to preach anywhere, especially not where healing was the topic. And, anyway, where was God when I needed Him, and where, in fact, was all this power I kept talking about?

To make matters worse, a certain lady who worked at the church had a son about my age, a precious young man who suffered from Down's syndrome. He had the IQ of a six-year-old. That night he was determined to play cowboys and Indians before the service started. I cajoled and coaxed and commanded, but all to no avail. Jimmy was unmoved.

A large man with a huge ten-gallon hat, an absurd sheriff's badge the size of a saucer, and twin plastic six-shooters, Jimmy was an apparition. He would crawl around under the pews in that darkened auditorium, sneaking up on me, then leap to his feet like a demonic jack-in-the-box, screaming "Bang, bang, Brudder Mark. Bang, bang!" It was absolutely terrifying, and his timing was flawless. Every time, just when I had become convinced he was gone at last, he would pop up with that blood-curdling, speech-impaired war cry.

"Bang, bang, Brudder Mark."

After only a few times being thus shot dead by this ludicrous "sheriff," Brudder Mark was just about ready to shoot back. In the midst of my misery, the Lord added insult to injury. A thought burst into my mind, so sudden and unbidden that I thought perhaps it was the Lord: *Why don't you ask Jimmy to pray for your foot?*

"Lord," I argued, "look at him. I have an earned doctorate and an IQ of 152. He's wearing a sheriff's badge!"

"Fine," the answer came, "it's your foot."

Then followed that awful silence, the one where you sense God is through discussing it.

"Jimmy," I beckoned to him, "come here."

He stood before me as sober as a judge, his cowboy hat so low that his ears stuck out like the handles on a soup mug.

"Yeth," he lisped.

"Jimmy, when you hurt yourself, does your mother pray for you?"

"Yeth, sir, she doth."

"Well, Jimmy, I have hurt my foot. Will you pray for me?"

Without a moment's hesitation, the massive cowpoke dropped to his knees and cradled my shoeless foot in his lap.

"Lord Jethuth, Brudder Mark have hurt him foot. Pweath, Jethuth, pweath heal him. In Jethuth name, amen."

With that he carefully put my foot back on the pew, leapt to his feet, drew both revolvers, and shot me again.

"Bang, bang, Brudder Mark!"

What is that? Pray for me and shoot me in the face. What *is* that? I have never felt less prayed for, less healed, or less helped in an hour of need.

Within twenty minutes that plantar wart was healed. It was gone, utterly, leaving no trace of itself, no tenderness, no swelling, nothing to remind my body that only minutes before it had been in excruciating pain. Yet when I found Jimmy in the church kitchen scarfing down ice cream, he was so limited intellectually that I could not seem to explain to him the miracle in which God had used him. He was infinitely more interested in the small mountain of butter pecan ice cream than he was in my story.

What is the lesson? Shall we find Jimmy, get a band and a van, and put him on the road? I can see it now: "The Sheriff Jimmy Healing Crusade." God forbid! Every time God grants a miracle He runs the risk of spawning a "ministry."

The point is that in that moment, a sweet, genuine

moment of authentic grace, God used an absolutely powerless instrument through whom He could manifest His healing power. There was naught of Jimmy to get in the way. His intellect formed no obstruction, and his ego laid claim on nothing. It was God's moment, God's glory, and God's power.

The strength of God, made perfect in Jimmy's weakness, became the precious healing ointment, the very balm of Gilead, poured not just on my hurting heel, but also on my wounded spirit. Jimmy, God through Jimmy, undid the damage done by an arrogant, manipulative self-promoter whose assistants tried to stage a miracle. It was not simply that my faith in miracles was restored. It was that Jimmy taught me the most enduring lesson of my life about power.

When Jesus spoke of *power*, and peace for that matter, He had to use human vocabulary, but the words could hardly bear the weight laid upon them. He promised them power, but not any kind of power they had ever seen. He meant *power*, not power.

THE GREATEST IPO
IN HISTORY

We struggle with this same problem ourselves every time we try to convey "God" thoughts in human words. At funerals we speak of going "up" to heaven when we die. Symbolically correct but not theologically, we use the word up because it works. Heaven is not up; it's *up*. The contrast is not geographical but dimensional. Heaven is above, higher, more perfect than anything we have ever experienced "down" here in the physical dimension. If heaven is straight up from, say New York, it is straight down from Sydney. The poor unfortunate who dies in Australia must, one supposes, circle the globe before ascending.

Down works the same way. Where is hell? Under our feet? If we drilled straight down from Kansas City, would we pop out in hell? No…in Calcutta. Hell is the shrinking away, the loss of all that is good and godly, until, as C. S. Lewis wrote, every spirit that has ever or will ever go to hell could fit in a crack in the sidewalk. Hell is not down. It's *down*.

Years ago the story circulated in some evangelical circles that in a mineshaft in Lithuania or some such place, screams and extreme heat were detected. This, then, was the mouth of hell, the story went. Do we honestly think that the mouth of hell is a Balkan mineshaft? That would surely simplify evangelism. A few hundred yards of concrete, and no one could ever go to hell again. Just seal that sucker up and forget it forever. Please!

There is no place in Scripture where this communication breakdown has caused the church as much heartache as Acts 1. Having longed for a new

Davidic kingdom, a messianic dominion with Jerusalem as its headquarters and them as its deputies, the disciples found their hopes dashed at the death of Jesus. His Resurrection likewise raised from the dead their dreams of kingdom and power and glory. *Now,* they thought, *now comes the kingdom.*

"Lord, wilt thou at this time restore the kingdom to Israel?"

They wanted the yoke of Gentile oppression snapped, the Romans defeated, and the glory of David renewed. Surely with Jesus having defeated death, the kingdom was now, and they wanted in on the ground floor. It was the greatest IPO in history, and they were the eleven original stockholders. The smell of power was a sweet perfume in their expectant nostrils.

This confusion has haunted the church for two thousand years and continues to until this day. On the eve of a crucial battle near Rome with his opponent Maxentius, the pagan emperor Constantine claims to have seen a vision, a cross in the sky with the words *in hoc signo vinces,* "In this sign you will win."[1]

The emperor promptly ordered his army to paint white crosses on their shields. When victory was his on the next day, Constantine ordered mass baptisms,

---

1. Gospelnet.com, "A Vision of Triumph: Constantine Wins the Day for Christianity," *Glimpses* 12, http://www.gospelcom.net/chi/GLIMPSEF/Glimpses/glmps012.shtml (accessed October 3, 2003).

and Christianity became the state religion of the Roman Empire. Constantine himself, however, was baptized only on his deathbed twenty-five years later.[2] Presumably he wanted to keep his options open while not offending the source of his victory, a fascinatingly modern approach.

None of this is to say that Constantine heard no voice and saw no vision of the cross. Both may well have been real, but, assuming they were, perhaps Constantine misunderstood their meaning. Just possibly God was telling Constantine that there is another way to power other than by conquest, another means to victory other than the sword, and that the way of the cross may lead, not to an empire, but into the kingdom. *Power*, not power.

THE POWER OF ROMAN LOGIC

No stranger to politics, the governor was raised in a city where malevolent power was exercised to smash lives and careers. Rome's armies, the most powerful in the world, crushed countries and cultures, not with intrigue, but with a brutality unmitigated by any hint of mercy. Though not named per se among Rome's pantheon of gods, power, not Zeus, ruled supreme. Rome meant power in the world as he knew it, only Rome, nothing else, nothing less, only Rome. In the

---

2. Ibid.

whole world there was no other power worth mentioning. Rome meant power, and in Palestine, at least, Pontius Pilate meant Rome.

That was precisely what concerned Governor Pilate the most about this case. Power was, as always, the only real issue, but his early education in Roman infighting and its dangerous political machinations had not prepared him for the ceaseless bickering of these Jews. The gods knew he had tried to understand, had listened patiently to rambling lectures on the nuanced distinctions of their major religious cults and political rivalries. Pharisees vs. Sadducees. Both vs. the Herodians. Squabbles *ad nauseum* to be sure, but meaningless in light of the bald fact that none of them had even a pinch of power except what Rome allowed. To Pilate they were petulant children arguing over borrowed toys in the back bedroom of a vast estate owned by a distant landlord. Beyond all that, they were unspeakably rude, unruly, implacable, and unfailingly resistant to clear Roman logic.

He had no clue why he had been posted here. Quirinius, his classmate who had been sent to Syria to govern there, commiserated, but no appeal was possible. "Judea," his orders said. "Procurator, Governor Regent, of the territories and peoples thereof in the name of the senate, the republic, and Caesar."

This maddening people, their incomprehensible customs, their barbaric religion so impoverished it could afford only a single god, and their barren, rocky land filled with barren, rocky fanatics made him ache for Rome and his father's house. He had wanted foreign service, trained for it, even petitioned the senate for it at no small expense, and he had been excited at his first provincial governorship. Now…O Zeus, now he just wanted to go home and leave these Jews to stew in their own juice.

"Governor?" The adjutant's smooth, warm voice and excellent Latin always comforted Pilate, reassured him that somewhere there was sanity, culture, and Roman civilization. "Governor, they won't go away. They demand to be heard."

"They demand. Perfect. Never in history have the conquered demanded so much, so arrogantly of their masters. Mark my words, Claudius, someday Rome will be forced to raze this country to the ground."

"Yes, Governor."

"Mark my words."

"Of course, Governor, I'm sure you're right. Only…"

"Only what?"

"What shall I tell them today?"

The governor sighed heavily and raked his manicured fingers through his prematurely thinning hair. His wife said baldness made him look more dignified, rather like the busts of the great Julius. She thought a governor should look like Caesar. Perhaps, but here in this dusty, remote, rock garden of Judea, Governor Pontius Pilate longed for more of Caesar's power and less of his dignity.

"Well, there's nothing for it, I suppose," Pilate said with weary resignation. "Send them in."

"Actually, Governor, you see...that's the thing of it. They won't come in."

"Won't come in?"

"It's their Passover. If they come in the house of Gentiles, they will be—uh..."

"Yes, yes. Unclean. What arrogance. Do you think they don't realize how insulting that is?"

"I should think, Sir, that they don't care. I have set up an official desk and chair on the courtyard pavement. Will you wear your formal robes?"

"No," the governor snapped, mildly irritated that his adjutant had assumed he would go out to meet with the Jewish elders. "Get my breastplate. I'll go out in full military garb. That should rile them. And get my dress sword. Perhaps a sword on my side will remind them who wields the power in this country. What is this about anyway? If they are in such a hurry that it can't wait until after their own feast, it must be important."

"They've arrested a false prophet."

The governor moaned. In this insane land prophets were more dangerous than swords, and more numerous.

"Must I get involved? Are you sure this is necessary, Claudius?"

"They want him executed."

"I do not understand these people. Do they love their prophets or hate them? They kill them all. It is safer to be a gladiator in Rome than a prophet in Jerusalem."

"Still, Governor, that's what they want."

"Life and death are Caesar's alone. Now they need Rome to kill their prophet. The power to kill is Rome's, and they know it. For His sake, this prophet had better remember it, too. This is not about prophecy. This is about power. What is His name anyway?"

"Jesus bar Joseph, from Nazareth."

"Ah, a Galilean. I hope he's not one of these sanctimonious Pharisees. Galileans tend to have more respect for real power than these Judeans."

"Remember, Governor, He is a prophet."

"I dread this whole thing."

On the portico, Governor Pontius Pilate—Roman citizen, Caesarean appointee, and plenipotentiary of the empire—stared in amazement at the pathetic figure before him. What power in this Jesus of Nazareth engendered such hatred from His own people? He had no army, was not even accused of having one, and had fomented no rebellion. Unarmed, taken with no struggle to speak of, friendless, countryless, and defenseless, the man seemed to stand outside the entire proceedings as if it had nothing to do with Him. His own countrymen were screaming for His blood. He had been tortured, beaten, and sleep-deprived, yet somehow the man remained calm, aloof, even detached. Indeed, He refused to respond, defend Himself, or even deny the charges, such as they were.

The Hebrew leaders said Jesus claimed to be a god. This amused Pilate. In Rome there were gods, demigods, and self-proclaimed gods galore. Caesar was a god, and his wife a goddess. *In Rome,* he thought, *we do not kill our gods—or worship them.*

This God, this beaten and bloody Jewish God was certainly silent before His captors and accusers. The governor had seen the accused, guilty and innocent alike, in a thousand legal venues, and they invariably rushed to their own defense. This Jesus would not open His mouth or offer evidence or even plead for His life. The governor's curiosity, more than his conscience, compelled him to seek a better understanding of this strange man, hated by so many, yet seemingly disengaged from the process that had the power to take His life.

"Do you not realize," Pilate demanded, "that I have the power to have You killed or to spare Your life?"

Jesus lifted His eyes to meet the governor's. At last a response. When it came, the Jew's answer astonished Pilate.

"You have no power over Me at all, none, except that which you are permitted by heaven to have."

Suddenly the governor found himself reluctant to allow this man's death. Something in His answer, cryptic as it was, or something in His eyes made Pilate want to release Him. Pilate was not entirely certain of who this Jesus was or even who He claimed to be. What was apparent was that the petty power brokers among the Sanhedrin's leadership had no understanding at all of this man's concept of power. The Roman world was all about power. Caesar had power. Pontius Pilate himself had some power. These scribes and Pharisees bickered over the crumbs of power under Caesar's table. Herod had power, of a sort, and used it without remorse to crush his enemies. One man in Israel who had absolutely no power was this ragged rabbi from the Galilee, yet He seemed more confident, more assured of His power than any of them.

The governor returned the rabbi's gaze but offered no response. How could he respond? What answer could he give? It was apparent that this man, insane or touched by the gods, was using the same vocabulary as Pilate and the others, but the words did not mean the same thing. Anyway, it was refreshing to meet someone, anyone, even a benign maniac that had no interest in personal power and who apparently believed that the governor's power came from heaven. That, at least, was unique. In that moment, the governor determined to use his power, however little he had, to spare this poor mystic's life.

THE SOUL OF SADDAM

This world is obsessed with governmental power, deriving from and depending upon the state, from an election, or succession, or even a military coup. Such power is positional and always temporary. In other words, as long as the office is yours, the power is yours. *Sic gloria transit mundi*, which loosely translated means, "Lose the election, and the phone stops ringing."

Power is inherent in the office. Only the character of the person in power varies its exercise. Idi Amin used power to ravish Uganda, Saddam Hussein to terrorize the world, and George Washington to build a republic. That is both the promise and the danger of persons in positions of power, and the reason that conscience and character as well as competence must be considered by a thoughtful electorate. The power of any position, say, the presidency of the United States, is there no matter who occupies the oval office. A moral pygmy may use it to cover his own weaknesses or even his crimes. A giant shoulders the awful weight of monumental positional power, not in eager frivolity, but in sobriety and in the fear of God.

Jesus' words to Pontius Pilate should be carved

over the doors of the White House, the Congress, and into the heart of every office holder.

> Jesus answered, Thou couldest have no power at all against me, except it were given thee from above.
>
> —JOHN 19:11

The paradox of positional power is that its dimensions mean little to those who wield it. In fact, the tinier the terrain, the smaller the office, the more immediate the temptation to tyranny. For one thing, the world watches the really grand offices. Under the constant gaze of the United Kingdom, and indeed the world, England's prime minister may find outward, if not inward, motivation to act nobly, to use his power for the common good. A bank teller, on the other hand, with no one watching, may mercilessly terrorize a confused elderly customer.

That desk, that one little window in that one branch bank is her domain, and she will brook no rebellion. Humorless, cold, demanding, and ruthlessly legalistic, she reminds the world and, more importantly, herself with every transaction that in her small corner of the kingdom of mammon, she rules supreme. What angry customers fail to understand is that every sullen confrontation, every refusal of service, every time she makes their transaction more difficult, awkward, and painful, the whole point is power. They wonder why she is making such a federal case out of this tiny detail or that procedural technicality. They do not understand. To her it is not a federal case. It is a cosmic case. The issue is not the order in which things are done. The real issue is her power, her realm, and her cold control, which reminds her that, though powerless in the rest of the world, in this tiny domain, she rules supreme.

It was the spirit of power that killed Jesus. Power is, in fact, the very essence of the spirit of antichrist. Antichrist does not mean "opposed to Christ," but rather, "an alternative Christ." When petty men in government and religion who had clawed their way up the corridors of power at last encountered the genuine Man of Power, He had to die. His life, His power, which denied theirs, refused to bow, to even give an answer. Power against power. His death was inevitable.

Herod killed all the male babies in Bethlehem because he feared the birth of the true king. He feared it because he did not understand it. Jesus did not want to be king as Herod was king. Content for Herod to be king, Jesus wanted to be *king*. Jesus never called for the downfall of Herod or Pilate or the Sanhedrin. They wanted, lusted for, clung to, and killed for power. Jesus never wanted power and never had any. He was a *king* but never a king. He had *power* but never power. Likewise it was *power*, not power He promised believers.

There is a mystery spirit of power—corrupting, evil, and able to rationalize, incite, and fuel any violence, every monstrosity, without a flicker of conscience or hesitation. To stay in power, ruthless men will destroy the lives of others, perjure themselves, do murder, and commit treason. The same spirit that motivated Herod and Pharaoh to commit genocide compels a president to lie on camera. Power is an addictive tyrant determined to sear consciences, sully souls, and strangle every impulse to do right.

Those who will do anything to gain power cannot be trusted with it. Those who will do anything to keep it are to be greatly feared and will be removed only at a terrible expense. Until the last moment, after all rational hope is gone, right up to the final second, the Saddam Husseins and Hitlers of this world will be quite willing to see their countries devastated and their armies decimated rather than give up one shred of their last grip on power.

The remarkable mystery about this nefarious spirit of power is that it steals the soul of a petty bureaucrat no less than that of dictator. That bank teller's domain, over which she rules as sovereign potentate, as tiny and insignificant as it may seem to others, is, nonetheless, hers. Failure to understand that has caused more than one to stand before her desk appealing to reason where reason is despised and futilely hoping for service from the soul of Saddam Hussein.

The smaller the kingdom, the pettier the despot. The great and benevolent monarch of a vast domain sees no threat in the request for a variance in some regulation touching only one square centimeter far, far below him. Not so the guardian of its governing regulations. Those rules, those precious technicalities over which she presides, mean all the world to her. Whatever customer, applicant, or petitioner stands before her mistakenly believes his request is the central issue of the moment. Not to her. For her the glorious opportunity to reassure herself that she is in full control is alpha and omega. That alone is all she cares about. Granting the request or denying it is all the same to her. Like the absurd knight guarding the bridge in *Monty Python and the Holy Grail*, she will listen to no logic, yield to no reason, and suffer no rebellion.

"None shall pass!" is her only and most passionate response to every comer. Even if she allows one to cross alive, the issue is still the same. The bridge is hers. Using the regulations as a broad sword, she alone is the cosmic permission-giver at that bridge. The bridge may be all she has, but she will kill for it, and woe to the knight who thinks his opinions or title or special needs mean anything.

The tyrants, the petty, nasty despots who rule bureaucratic desks and commercial cash registers see every client and customer as an opportunity to wield power. Their unreasonableness, their intractable devotion to the rules makes every transaction a war. Having won or lost, each enemy leaves the field of combat asking the same befuddled question. *What was that about?*

Power. Always, ever there is only one issue. Who is in charge here? Power is the only question.

WITCHES WITHOUT FEATHERS

When, after a long recess in missions, I came back to pastor again in America, I was asked not infrequently if I was ever afraid in Africa. My answer was always, "Not so desperately or so often as I am now." If you want to be really afraid, pastor an American megachurch. In Africa, all the witches wear feathers. It is in church where you can't tell the players without a program.

Power games have gutted churches, destroyed ministries, and left the wives and children of pastors in quivering dysfunction. These "games" played by ruthless, remorseless rebels are nothing other or less than witchcraft in all its evil. There is a bitter irony in evangelicals up in arms over Harry Potter yet willing to tolerate without a murmur witchcraft in the choir loft.

Witchcraft is the manipulation of spiritual forces through natural means in order to achieve a desired end. Some elements must be in place for witchcraft to work: a controllable subject, a manipulative "priest," and some control mechanism, usually an idol. If the subject will not be controlled, that is to say, cannot be intimidated, frightened, or manipulated, the power of the witch is useless. Lose the control, lose the subject, lose the power. That is the secret of defeating witchcraft.

> The curse causeless shall not come.
> —PROVERBS 26:2

In Africa I always teach that the blood and priesthood of Jesus protect us utterly from the blood and priesthood of witches, because perfect love casts out all fear, and the control mechanism of witchcraft is fear. Fear gone, witchcraft cannot curse us, hurt us, hinder us, or control us. Why then does witchcraft work in the choir loft?

The controlling idol, the mechanism of manipulation in the modern American church is "friendship." The controlling fear is loss of position and relationship. The inner circle of witchcraft admits candidates only on probation to an office in the choir cabinet, perhaps, or acceptance into some elite level of leadership. This is reinforced with rewards such as dinner at the choir director's house or a ski retreat with the senior leadership. Heady stuff, indeed, the loss of which would be grievous. Such perks can, therefore, become a controlling idol.

Witchcraft is about power, power to control the outcome, others, natural forces, or demons. It is a refusal to submit to God, to wait on Him, or to let Him determine the outcome. Witchcraft is the seizure of power illegitimately, the appropriation of that which is under God's sovereign authority. Charms, spells, the stars, or magic crystals are all bypasses circumventing the will, purpose, plan, and timing of God. To know what is His alone to know and to bypass His will in the lives of others are witchcraft and rebellion against God's authority.

That is the reason the Bible says, "For rebellion is as the sin of witchcraft" (1 Sam. 15:23). There is fundamentally no difference between the teenager who will not obey her mother, the board member who gossips about the pastor, and the wizard whose spells are designed to bring sickness upon his enemies. Rebellion and witchcraft are the twin sisters of darkest evil.

Furthermore, there is no "white" witchcraft. The fallacious premise of "good" witchcraft is that the motivation justifies the magic. Never. The witch who works a spell to make some boy love a certain girl claims innocence by comparison with the witch whose spells kill boys and girls. The distinction fails because rebellion, not results, is the issue. If a girl cannot will the desired boy to love her, and prayer fails, and God will not move, then what is the harm, she asks, in a little innocent love potion? Much harm in every way—the lack of faith, an unwillingness to trust, a refusal to wait, and rebellion against the manifest will of God spell witchcraft. No good motive can make it otherwise.

A businessman in a church I pastored used his adult Sunday school class to recruit members for a breakaway church. He twisted my words, quoted me out of context, and finally rejected the authority of the board. In a decision where the legitimate authority of the church ruled against him, he incited a knot of malcontents, excusing all his lies, false accusations, and rebellion as necessary because the pastor and board would not listen to God.

Another businessman in my church said, "Well, Dr. Rutland, he is a hard-headed man."

"No," I responded, "he is a witch."

JEZEBEL

The letter was a forgery. The seal of the king, the royal emblem stamped boldly into the molten wax was genuine enough. That the message purported to be from the king himself was the obvious deception. The village elders stared balefully at the letter open before them on the table and avoided each other's eyes. This was Jezebel's doing.

King Ahab was neither clever enough nor bold enough to send such a directive. The letter was painfully obvious. They were to suborn sufficient perjured testimony against Naboth to convict him of treason and blasphemy, both punishable by death, and stone him. They knew that should they refuse, death would find them as well. Naboth was a good man, an honorable man from a respected family. They willed him no ill. But Jezebel did. Naboth would die, had to die, and his vineyards would be appropriated by the state; there was nothing anyone could do about it. Why should they die with him? Why should their families lose all when Naboth was doomed anyway?

King Ahab could stop this. *Perhaps,* they thought, *perhaps we should appeal to him for clarification, or even verification, make him claim the letter and restate its murderous intent.* No, that was useless. Even if Ahab denied knowledge of the letter, Naboth would still die. Oh, an investigation into the forgery would be launched with great bluster and then be forgotten. Some other charge would be leveled at Naboth, and in the process, they would have made an enemy, a terrible, fearsome enemy of the most powerful person in the kingdom. Jezebel was behind this even as she was behind all the real power in Ahab's kingdom. From behind the curtain, silent, lethal, and conscienceless, she manipulated the weak, intimidated the cowardly, and crushed the righteous without remorse. Ahab? He was nothing, a king in name only, a sensual, petulant, spoiled brat who wanted the throne and all its pleasures but cared little for the power. That he ceded to Jezebel, willing for her to use it any way she wanted, just so long as he got what he wanted. Naboth's vineyard was all Ahab wanted. Life in peace was all the elders wanted. Power was what Jezebel wanted.

DEATH AND COWARDS

The spirit of Jezebel, so-called, has been frequently misapprehended as being about sexual immorality. The phrase "a painted Jezebel" actually uses her bloody name in vain. She may have been promiscuous, as pagans tend to be—and she was pagan not Jewish—but, for a Jezebel, power, not sex, is the prize.

A Jezebel may or may not covet a public office, except as it brings power. A Jezebel spirit more often hides behind the scenery, manipulating the outcome with dangerous dexterity. The MO of a modern Jezebel spirit is not unlike the prototype. Perjury may be suborned, lies and gossip used viciously, and ultimately any obstruction, life, leader, or pastor that refuses to yield to her power will be destroyed one way or another. Remember, Naboth's vineyard was immaterial to her except that it afforded her the perfect opportunity to remind her husband, his subjects, and herself who the real power broker was.

Imagine a White House with a weak and carnal president, controlled and manipulated by a vicious first lady willing to let him have or do anything as long as she wielded the real power. The result would be predictable. There would be scandal, lying, perjury, and a rose garden full of dead bodies. What a ghastly thought! God forbid that should ever happen in America.

It does, however, happen altogether too frequently in all kinds of organizations, including the local church. Wherever the weak suffer backroom manipulators to spread gossip, bring down leadership, and destroy reputations for power's sake, churches come under the evil sway of a Jezebel spirit.

A person with a Jezebel spirit need not be a woman. A Jezebel spirit is not gender specific. A Jezebel requires only two things to operate—the cover of darkness and the weakness of others. Wherever a Jezebel spirit is found, it is there because it is allowed to be. Serious evil and blatant lies, as well as other rebellious and manipulative acts of social terrorism, can easily be rationalized by Jezebel. Well camouflaged with religious language and serving some noble cause, every kind of backroom wickedness will be her stock in trade.

Jezebel depends on the weak and self-serving in positions of authority combined with a cowardly unwillingness to expose her. This is the "wing of bat and eye of newt" by which Jezebel's witchcraft works.

Public exposure always breaks the spell, but that requires courage, more courage than is common among some church members.

If the elders of Naboth's village had denounced the letter from Jezebel as the forgery it was, Naboth might have been spared. They knew, however—and were quite right—that Jezebel would resort to murder and mayhem if she had to. Wherever there is a weak king or president and a hidden Jezebel spirit operating behind the scenes, dead bodies will begin to pile up around them. Ahab and Jezebel will always be surrounded by death and by cowards.

SIMON

The message Philip preached, the message of the gospel had moved Simon, deeply moved him. He, like the rest of Samaria, had accepted Jesus as the long-awaited One and had been baptized. The forgiveness Philip proffered in the name of Jesus was wonderful to Simon as it was to all the Samaritans. Everything in Simon's life was better. Even the deception and manipulation and sorcery were gone. Why, then, was he not happy?

Simon told himself that he was not bothered by his loss of celebrity. Since Philip brought Jesus to town he had become Simon—not Simon Magus, not

Simon the Sorcerer, just Simon. He told himself he was perfectly happy to be only one among many of the new believers in Samaria. Well, not happy, perhaps, but content, certainly, to surrender to Jesus and Philip the prominence he had so desperately sought.

Then came Peter and John, and the bothersome grain of sand in Simon's sandal became an unbearable agony. Jesus, Philip, Peter, John, the Holy Spirit—where did Simon fit? It seemed that everyone had a place in the light except Simon. Philip had taught them that Jesus blessed and prospered His followers, but in fact, Jesus had cost Simon everything of any importance.

Before Jesus came to Samaria the people had looked to Simon, had believed in him, and had thrilled to his legerdemain. They had also been willing to pay. Now Simon had lost face, forfeited his prominence in the community, and seen his river of revenue dry up. The Samaritans had no more need of magic tricks since Philip's miracles were apparently not tricks at all. Now with Peter and John bestowing the Holy Spirit with but a touch, Simon's power as well as his position were unwanted and unneeded. In fact, because their power, the power of the Holy Spirit, was real, Simon's "power" was now despised by all, including Simon himself, as the counterfeit it was.

Simon would miss the income, but, then again, he had saved up money enough for a long time to come. It was the power that he longed for. The lonely, the needy, the sick, and the vengeful had looked to him before Jesus came to Samaria. Simon—not Jesus, Philip, or Peter—had been the source of spiritual power. That delicious, salacious moment when a barren woman or a bankrupt merchant had implored his help would never come again. Now they all looked to Jesus, and Simon was but another foot soldier. Jesus' preeminence was obvious, Philip's miraculous power was manifest, and Peter and John were apostles with the power of apostles. Where, but as a face in the crowd, was there a place for Simon?

Then there appeared a ray of light, a revelation moment when the dark clouds parted and the sun shone through to show Simon the way back to power and position. He watched as Peter and John laid their hands on the heads of longing seekers, and he saw empty lives filled dramatically, not only with life and love, but also with gratitude to Peter and John. There it was. That was what he wanted, what, in fact, he had enjoyed before they arrived. He wanted those humble, imploring eyes fixed once again on him. He wanted the gratitude and the admiration.

He saw his opportunity and chuckled to himself to realize how close he had come to missing the point. Peter and John were not so different from Simon himself. At the end of the day they wanted what he wanted, and they enjoyed it no less. The power of the Holy Spirit in the lives of his fellow Samaritans was obvious, but, in a sense, it made them all powerful in the same way, at the same level. That pedestrian power was not enough for men like Simon. The power to grant or, in fact, withhold the power—ah, that was different. That was what Peter and John had and what Simon wanted. He now knew, now understood who Peter and John really were, how like him they were, and how to approach them became, in the light of that knowledge, quite obvious.

"How much?" Simon asked the big Galilean. "How much will it take to do what you do? Name your price. I am through with magic, and I can see that this Holy Spirit is real. Bestowal authority is what I want. Give me this power that on whom I lay my hands, they may receive the Holy Spirit."

Peter's eyes, filled with fury, told Simon he had made a terrible mistake. The big man's face flushed with anger, and for a moment Simon thought Peter might strike him. But why? Money for power was a fair exchange. Why was Peter so angry? They were alike, so alike, both wanting the same thing, and both aware of how to get it. Why all the anger?

THE HOPE TO CONTROL

Through that power by which we have been controlled we may hope to control others. That is the temptation of Jezebel and Simon, of witchcraft of every kind. He who is mercenary at heart will use money to turn the hearts of others. The fearful, hoping to make others afraid, resort quickly to threats and intimidation. The Pharisees who lived in bondage to legalism, hair splitting, and word baiting were sure the same tactics would work on Jesus. In our fallenness we tend to project our own weakness onto others, confident that whatever controls us will control them.

Where Simon the Magician went wrong with Simon the Apostle was in projecting his own weakness onto a man whose frailties ran in other directions. Peter had been, before Pentecost at least, easily intimidated, but money had never been his problem. Simon the Sorcerer would have done well to check into the deaths of Ananias and Sapphira before attempting to manipulate Simon Peter with money.

THE DEVOURING MYSTERY

The sons of Babylon are the hunters of men who revel in violence. Having drunk from the river that flows from the heart of mystery Babylon, they are forever captive to its narcotic sorcery. The ability to deny, to withhold, or even to kill, once tasted, becomes the liquor for which they will do anything and without which they refuse to live. Even the smallest droplet of this potent potion makes imbibers into slaves.

Xerxes and Alexander were slaves. So were the

Caesars and the Czars and the Pharaohs. In gripping power they were gripped; in seizing they were seized until the power that made them at last unmade them without a trace of mercy. As they lived, and then died, by the sword, power stole first their lives, then their very personhood. They became half souls, undone spirits without lives or relationships or inner selves. They lost themselves to power and, like all addicts, became defined, corrupted, and erased by the very substance for which they lusted.

The ironic paradox of power, the hidden joke, is that while the world sees them as persons of power or, rather, persons *in* power, they lack power entirely. They are capable of much perhaps, but they are incapable of being fully alive *out* of power. Seeking significance by wielding power, they are wielded then tossed away.

The devouring mystery called *power* has little to do with the extent of its realm or its theater of operation. Power in a bishop's soul can corrupt no less thoroughly than in a king's, and a power-mad clerk owned by mystery Babylon is as terrible a tyrant as there is. A bishop may control his subjects with manipulation and deception rather than a firing squad, but power is power. The clerk may lack the opportunity to execute her victims, but she gleefully kills the joy of a dozen a day.

Outside of time, above the geopolitical and military systems that seem so very powerful, Jesus stands unchanged, unthreatened, and undiminished. This world's power is but the power of mystery Babylon, and Babylon the great is fallen, *is fallen.*

His power, when Babylon is no more, shall remain, for He is I AM beyond time.

PART II

That Pure Power

But ye shall receive power, after that the Holy Ghost is come upon you: and ye shall be witnesses unto me both in Jerusalem, and in all Judea, and in Samaria, and unto the uttermost part of the earth.

—ACTS 1:8

THE UNSILENCED SONG

Behind the conspicuous din of power, unceasing and undaunted, another sweeter sound is often heard. Drowned out, seemingly silenced, it plays on, like the melody of a wren in competition with a passing truck. Throbbing, deafening engines roar past, overwhelming all else, filling the air with an adolescent, selfish noise until, quickly gone, the truck is forgotten by the breeze. Out of ear, out of mind, so to speak.

Then the song is heard again, a captivating trill all full of life and joy. Overquilted briefly by the crude mechanical roar of the truck, perhaps intimidated, did the tiny creature wait its turn? Or did it sing on, uncrushed, full of irrepressible song, not waiting to be enjoyed to enjoy itself?

The latter is surely true. The truck, passing in a blaring riot of unrepentant noise, is mindless of the bird and the heartrending beauty of its song. Yet the wren sings on. Once the truck is gone, carrying its awful nose with it, the purest melody of nature comes unmasked, but it was always there.

Another kind of power, like Babylon a mystery, but, unlike Babylon, with no lust for blood, has ever been, is yet, undiminished and unsilenced. For every Pharaoh there was a Moses, meek and unseduced by the corridors of power. In the court of every Xerxes lived an Esther who wielded not a scepter or a sword, but influence.

They were always there. Cupbearers, shepherd boys, and prophets without portfolio, they were moved by a power far greater than any king's. Throneless and crownless for the most part, their power derived not from position or title, but from an unction only rarely poured upon the heads of kings or presidents.

From Babylon and Calvary two rivers flow. Both mysterious, each has the power to change the souls of all they touch. To drink from Babylon's surging tide, men strive and kill and give all they have. Then having stood but for a moment, for the flick of an eyelid in the splendid light of worldly power, they find, at last, unhappiness and empty death.

From a distant cross where a lonely figure in agony dies unheralded and despised, there flows another river of undiluted, unalloyed power far greater than any Caesar ever knew. That stream heals and makes the dead to live. Those who kneel and drink from that stream will find the power to break kings in pieces and tear down forts, to make the weary dance with joy and set the captive free.

THE POWER OF SERVANTHOOD

"Do you wish to be the greatest in My kingdom?" The Master's question was direct, breath-catchingly direct, and upon the tender flesh of their innermost unspoken desires it fell like a glowing coal. Unprepared, they hesitated momentarily, but their eyes revealed the desperate passion in their minds. No moderated tone, no downcast eyes, no contrived reticence could hope to hide the truth. Beyond their power to express it, more certainly than they wanted the Master to know, being great was the wonderful unattainable for such as they.

Never having known greatness, never having tasted power over more than a leaky fishing boat, they longed for it as impoverished children ache for the sweets of the wealthy. But a taste, but a crumb of the mysterious recipe, and they would know the secrets of the powerful. Until this pregnant moment, that which Herod and Caesar had tasted—the daily fare of magistrates, centurions, and priests—had been ever beyond their reach.

The promise in the Master's question, in His eyes, in the thick, portentous atmosphere of the room, drew them close. The light of lust was in their eyes, and their breath came quick and shallow. At last they were to know the unknowable, to possess the prize denied the poor and lowly, to be the men to whom others turned, to be bowed to and not to bow, to be feared and not to fear.

"What, Lord? Tell me the secret of greatness."

"Why you? Why should you be the greatest among us?"

"I said nothing about being the greatest."

"I am the eldest. I should be the greatest."

"I am the most educated in the Scriptures. Who can deny it? None of you. Let it be me, Lord. Tell them that I shall be Your deputy, and put the matter to rest."

Their bitter quibbling erupted without warning, filling the room with anger and turning their eyes momentarily on each other. Now they looked back to the Master, and, seeing in His eyes that strange faraway gaze they had come to know so well, they fell silent and waited, seething inwardly but saying nothing.

"The kings of this world would lord it over their subjects. Tyrants or benefactors, they still want the same thing."

"What, Lord? What do they want?"

"Control. But you are not to be so. Do you see how I serve you bread and wine? Who is greater—the servant or the served? You see that I serve you. Serve each other. That is the secret of greatness in My kingdom."

Rising from His seat, the Master took a basin of water and a towel and began to wash their feet.

"Like this," He said, as He knelt before them, taking their feet in His hands to bathe away the dirt. "Do it like this."

And they were ashamed.

THE SERVANT LEADER

The power of servant leadership lies not in position but in motive. The CEO of a massive corporation, holding great responsibility, may "wash his employees' feet" by seeking their benefit in business. There is no conflict between a well-managed business making a profit for its stockholders and one making a good life for its employees. There is no room for exploitation in Jesus' model of servant leadership.

The servant leader is still in authority even as Jesus was when He washed the disciples' feet. No one in the room doubted who the leader was. Because He authentically ministered to their needs, no one resigned, no respect was squandered, and no face was lost.

Servant fathers will still discipline their children. The servant CEO will still make decisions, sometimes decide for layoffs, and will dismiss employees who fail to meet company standards. He will never browbeat, threaten, or manipulate. He will not withhold money or praise or encouragement.

The servant leader stoops to anoint his followers with the oil of gladness and never stands taller than when he kneels to wash their feet. His power rests in servanthood, not in dominion. Far from losing power in serving, he is enriched by it. He goes from strength to strength not by bending others to his will, but by sacrificing that they might be blessed.

What does servant leadership really mean in practical terms for a CEO or a college president such as I am? Does it mean that the CEO is out in the parking lot washing his employees' cars every day? Does it mean that the college president makes the beds and cleans the bathrooms in the dorms?

No, it doesn't mean that. Not that I am too good for it, however, but if I spend my working hours doing that for which I am not paid, what I am paid to do goes undone. Then I would be stealing from the college. Jesus washed the disciples' feet once, and the fact that it is recorded is the surest proof that He did not do it every day.

Being a servant leader is about being genuinely interested in the well-being of those entrusted to you. It means treating subordinates with respect and securing the dignity of all. To reduce the Jesus model of servant leadership to random acts of servitude is to trivialize a great truth. To make footwashing merely ceremonial is to risk ritualizing the call to practical servanthood, thereby separating it from real life. Authentic servant leadership is indeed sacramental, and does, in fact, mean practical acts of kindness, but it is so much more.

Servanthood is a mysterious spirit with power sufficient to break proud hearts and humble the high and mighty. Infinitely more important for leaders than for servants, an attitude more than an action, the power of servanthood is very near who Jesus is and who He was on the last night before He was crucified. Loving Him, we grow like Him. Like Him we serve. Serving, we know His power. Empowered, we change and heal whom we serve.

THE TESTED BRIDE

The palm trees waving in the faint breeze welcomed him in from the desert. Squinting his tired old eyes, he could just make out the orange-tiled roofs of the houses and buildings of Padanaram. Only for Abraham would he have endured such a journey at his age. He should be sitting in a tent drinking tea and inflicting his memories upon his grandchildren, not traipsing off across an ocean of sand in search of a bride for his master's son.

Now that the caravan was at its destination, he prayed for God to answer his test. Abraham demanded that Isaac's bride be from among his own people. Isaac had very different concerns and had pressed them daintily upon the ancient ambassador, reminding his father's servant that practical concerns considered, beauty in a bride was not completely without importance. For Abraham a Semite, for Isaac a beauty;

how was he to make the choice? Hence the test that now, God be pleased, would find a bride, *the* bride, the *exact* bride for Isaac.

He did not dare to hope that the first girl he met would be of the household of Bethuel, a raving beauty for Isaac, and the very choice of God. He would test and keep on testing until he found her.

He and his men guided their camels in amongst the trees and began to dismount. Men and beasts groaned at the process and stared longingly at the deep well and empty troughs. Only when someone came with a rope and pitcher could they drink. Such implements as heavy pitchers were useless weight on a desert trek, but hospitality demanded that the keepers of the well supply them for travelers who came in peace.

Lithe and lovely, her dark eyes taking in the knot of men and quickly estimating that they were harmless, a girl approached with her pitcher upon her rounded shoulder. Swaying softly, she moved with a gracious, unaffected sensuality that stirred even an old man and made the young ones stare. Her smile, when he spoke to her, was the dawn of a glorious morning, and he envied the boy who would wake to it each day.

"Good evening, daughter."

"Good evening, uncle."

Her voice, her cinnamon skin, a sweet supple figure, and the gentle eyes of a dove—oh, to be seventy-five again. Don't be fooled, he reminded himself sternly. No fool like an old fool. Every girl looks beautiful after weeks in the desert sun. Was she of the tribe of Abraham? That first, then the test.

"Who is your family, daughter?"

"I am Rebekah, the daughter of Bethuel the son of Nahor." Blessed be the God of Abraham! He was impressed with her upbringing. She answered fully, adding nothing, and asking nothing in return. An insolent girl would have demanded his right to know, and an overly bold girl would certainly have had questions of her own.

Now the test. Don't jump to conclusions. Use the test. Let God confirm it.

"Will you give an old man a drink?"

"Of course, revered uncle. Rest yonder in the shade, and I will draw for you and your camels and your men."

Without another word she moved quickly—ah, the energy of youth—thoughtful of the thirsty throats of the men and their animals. He watched her bend and draw the water, strong for one so slim, and rejoiced that his test had been passed by this alluring child.

Reaching into his saddlebags he drew out two beautiful golden bracelets and, gently taking her small hand, slid them on her wrists. Then, slipping the ring onto the maiden's delicate finger, he let himself, at last, rejoice.

"God be praised. The God of Abraham has given me success. God be praised, indeed."

Confused and frightened, the girl turned and ran away, as any modest well-bred girl should. He laughed. She would be back. When her family saw the weight and purity of Abraham's gold, they would come to find him. He need only wait. Anyway, the girl had passed the test. The choice of God was made. That was that.

Now to drink and rest. Quick success meant the long journey home would start soon. Ah, Isaac, my boy, you are in for a blessing.

THE CAMELS YOU WATER

The test of Rebekah was the test of servanthood. The true bride of Isaac, or of Christ for that matter, is tested best by servanthood, not beauty. Rebekah, full of grace, not content to do only what was asked, went far beyond. Gracious servanthood always goes beyond, gives more, goes farther, and does more than the bare minimum.

Furthermore, she hurried. Not reluctantly, not dragging her feet, not with the posture of the put-upon, Rebekah hurried to serve. She knew the men and camels were thirsty, and she acted in haste out of concern for them.

To do more than is asked and to do it quickly with joyful energy is the mark of a true servant, a mark easily recognized by an old and trusted servant. It takes one to know one. Even more than that, however, it is the key to blessings.

As Rebekah labored away filling and refilling the trough, not easy work by the way, she had no idea what her act of servanthood would win for her. Remember, the camels you water may carry you to a blessing.

One day an elderly man, obviously a poor man, came into a Midwestern diner. A young waitress served him with such a kindly and sweet manner that he returned day after day for years. He came every day for breakfast at the diner, always ordered the same thing, and never tipped very big. He refused to allow anyone else to wait on him. As far as the townsfolk or the waitress knew, he had no family and no friends. His fondness for the young waitress was eccentric to say the least. Her fondness for him was inexplicable. When he died he had no one, not even a distant nephew, whom he might call his rightful heir. No one was more shocked than the waitress when his will was probated and she received a small fortune, one about which he had given not even the slightest hint.

She was not calculating. She did not somehow size him up as a closet millionaire and decide to take a chance on the "good deeds lotto." Hers was genuine kindness, "old-fashioned service with a smile" that proved yet again that it is still possible to do well by doing good.

Not every old dude with thirsty camels is the chance of a lifetime to snag a fortune or a husband. Yet every opportunity to serve is a demonstration of the mysterious power of servanthood. She who bends to serve is moving in a flow of mysterious power utterly incomprehensible to the world. The order of the towel and basin, whose founder we serve, is not the fellowship of the subjected. It is a whole new way of looking at power. It is demeaning to be forced to serve, but Jesus' new revelation was that nothing can be forced upon you for which you volunteer.

Throughout the extended Roman Empire one law in particular galled the oppressed peoples. Due to the heavy equipment he carried and the long marches, any Roman soldier could commandeer any bystander to carry part of his burden for one mile. This was economical to Rome, limiting the number of pack animals needed by its far-flung armies and helpful in keeping its armies mobile and fresh. It was, however, disruptive and humiliating to the occupied lands.

Jesus turned that boiling resentment on its head with His unique perspective on power. "Look," He explained, "if someone compels you to go a mile, you feel as though you have been demeaned, and you chafe at your lack of power. If you volunteer to carry a Roman's pack a second mile, if you go beyond what is demanded, and if you do it of your own free will, you are empowered far beyond him whose burden you heft. By law he can demand a mile. At that point he is 'in charge.' When you freely offer more than is the legal limit, you are back 'in charge.' You are now the stronger helping the weaker, the generous being gracious to the demanding and needy."

Jesus' whole concept of power was top-side down from that of the world systems. Governments, institutions, and armies depend on position, rank, and title to keep order and do business. That in itself is not evil. Someone must lead, direct, supervise, or teach. The dark and terrible mystery of power is always at work, however, to seduce leaders and executives and college presidents, to drag them down into the ersatz "power" of arrogance and exploitation and away from true servant leadership.

> Ye know that the princes of the Gentiles exercise dominion over them, and they that are great exercise authority over them. But it shall not be so among you: but whosoever will be great among you, let him be your minister; and whosoever will be chief among you, let him be your servant: even as the Son of Man came not to be ministered unto, but to minister, and to give his life a ransom for many.
> —MATTHEW 20:25–28

The spirit of Christ is the spirit of ministry. It is in serving, healing, blessing, and binding up that the children of the King most resemble their Father. This is not antiwealth, antileadership, or antiauthority. Jesus was not an anarchist. It is, however, about a new kind of power, a new way of seeing and wielding power that is *servantly* and full of God's care for the weak. The spirit of Babylon and of Rome is the lust for power, the power to lift up or sweep away, to own, to kill, and to make the lowly fear. Whether in a day laborer or a corporate king, the spirit of Christ is servanthood, ego-crucifying, self-denying, others-centered servanthood.

THE POWER OF GRACE

Hands—harsh, cruel hands—and voices even harsher filled the darkened room and shattered their stolen moment. Without a good-bye, flesh torn away from flesh, he was there no more, while she, alone and full of shame, was left to face their rage. Clutching at the bedclothes, hysteria clawing at her soul, she tried to cover herself, but they would not wait.

Out, nearly naked, into the street, fear lashing her along, closer to death with every step, dazed and hopeless, she staggered from the meaty slaps of those women who could reach her. So many people and so much anger disoriented her. The jolting transition from fevered embrace to feverish mob pushed her mind right to the brink of a snap. Where did they all come from? Why were they so angry?

Hurled at last to the dusty street, she lay as she landed, an unmoving, unresisting rag shredded by life and lust and law who, having hoped for love, now expected only death. Finding not even the mental energy to listen to the storm of voices raging back and forth above her, she clutched her gown to her and waited for the rain of rocks that would end the whole horrible nightmare.

Confused as she was, the shift in momentum around her made no sense. Gradually she became aware that silence reigned again; no…more than silence, peace. Of that, above all, she could make absolutely no sense at all. When the angry voices were still, and the street around her was empty, she lifted her eyes to search for an explanation. One man stood looking down at her. Behind Him a small knot of others, unfamiliar to her, studied her, not with rage or fear or even contempt, but with wonder.

"Where are they that condemn thee?"

"Gone, sir. All gone."

"Neither do I condemn thee."

At these words, at His eyes and voice, a surge of power, some sweet, wild force unknown to her, moved through her being like spring-chilled wine on a summer night. As though no condemnation but His mattered, His refusal to judge her was more than a way to elude a stoning she deserved. The power of it sweeping through her spirit and her body, far more wonderful than the most ecstatic embrace in a lover's arms, seemed somehow to make her feel clean and, strangest of all, clothed.

"Now, go your way and sin no more."

She turned to find and face her husband and her future and herself, not with grim resolve, but having encountered some cleansing, liberating power for which she had no name. As she walked, His last words filled her, consumed her like raging fire. Sin no more. *I won't*, she thought. *I won't.*

WHEN GOD SHOUTS: THE POWER OF GRACE

When I played high school football, the most vicious and lethal runner I ever tackled was the coach's son, Jared. I dreaded our intersquad practices more than any game because Jared played tailback, and I played defensive back. Having ripped through the line, Jared would burst into the secondary line like a Scud missile, all helmet and knees and demons. He was not the biggest guy I ever tackled, nor the fastest, nor even the strongest. He was the most punishing.

When I asked him about his secret, he demanded that I come to his house after school. This invitation or summons I found surprising, since, as far as I knew, no one on the team had ever been to Jared's house. In fact, as far as I knew, he hadn't a friend in the world, because he was not only a vicious and lethal runner, but a vicious and lethal human being.

Once inside his dark and stifling garage, Jared indicated an army of dents, waist high on the inside of the metal door, resembling for the entire world the work of a psycho with a sledgehammer.

"There's your answer," he said. "When I turned twelve, my coach-father put a helmet on my head and made me run into that door. For the last five years I've hit it every day. Christmas, New Year's, and birthdays included. Any day I didn't hit it hard enough to satisfy my dad, I had to go again and again until I did. You know, you run into a metal garage door 365 days a year for five years, a 150-pound cornerback just don't look like much."

No wonder he was such a vicious runner and such a vicious human being. I cannot begin to imagine the fear, frustration, and anger boiling around in a young boy, driven day after day to attempt the impossible. Knowing that regardless of how ferociously he should hurl himself against that unyielding aluminum barrier, he would succeed only in denting its metal hide and his own young ego. What interior hurt he must have sustained, and how, so driven by his father's unreasonable demands, he must have hated himself, his father, and even the very game he played so well.

Many believers labor under the tragic misperception that God is just such an unreasonable coach-father. They see themselves on one side of a massive and unmovable mountain striving desperately, frenetically, year after year to find a face-to-face relationship with God who waits not so patiently on the other side.

From the other side of the mountain, they fully expect to be berated. "Hit it again! Harder! Come on, you big sissy, pull your socks up and get back in the game!"

The voice never comes, not from God at least, but they dread it with such fearsome agony that in their pathetic attempts to avoid it, they slavishly hack away at the mountain or try to scale it or tunnel under it. At last all their pitiable efforts prove in vain, and the predictable anger, frustration, and fear ooze in over the threshold of their souls.

Having been saved by grace, such Christians are subsequently "dis-graced" by a work's righteousness, which is not only unchristian, but downright demonic. Demonic, because human power has been substituted for divine grace. Attempting to perfect themselves, they hammer in futility at the metal door of success and find only failure and self-condemnation.

In Zechariah 4:6, God denounces all such prideful dependence on human power.

That Pure Power

> Not by might, nor by power but by
> my spirit [grace] saith the LORD of
> hosts.

This is contrary to the self-help, self-sufficient, self-exalting self-worship of the contemporary Western mind. In their search for personal empowerment in every area of life, postmodern believers, true to the age in which they live, hope to find the right recipe of power to remove the mountain. In their diets and exercise programs they hope for physical perfection. They pore over magazine articles about finances, feast on books about relational empowerment, and harbor high hopes for the hot new word from an army of management and leadership gurus. They are, likewise, confident that they will find the correct formula of personal power to knock aside whatever mountainous hindrance, habit, sin, or stronghold stands between them and God.

They will not. The power to remove such mountains is not theirs but God's. He waits for them to face their impotence and let Him demonstrate His power, the only power that accomplishes what they cannot. As long as they choose to labor in their own strength, God will let them. When fatigued and stripped of all self-confidence, they collapse at the foot of the mountain and cry out for God to do what they cannot; power, divine and fully sufficient, is unleashed for their deliverance.

Some have mistakenly understood grace to be God's willingness for our mountains to remain, simply overlooked or excused or winked at by our grandpaw in the sky. That is the mayonnaise theory of grace—slap enough on, and even rancid ham will taste all right.

Grace, true grace, is not God's reluctant willingness for our mountains to remain. It is God's desire and power to remove them Himself!

We squander oceans of emotional and spiritual energy in our fear that God will shout at us. Yet when we finally give up, it is not at us that God shouts, but at the mountain we so despise. God is not the cosmic coach, screaming, "Do better." "Fast more." Or, "Cut that out."

When God shouts, the dreaded mountain of our dis-grace melts like wax, and we at last see Him face-to-face. The word of His power, the power to pluck up and pull down, is not a summons to put our shoulder to the wheel of law and roll it uphill. The word God shouts is the one word with power enough to pull up mountains like pesky weeds and toss them onto the rubbish heap of forgotten foes.

What God shouts is: *Grace! Grace!*

THE POWER OF GIVING

This is all that I have. You see? This bit of meal and enough oil to fry it in. I shall make the last falafel of my life, eat it with my child, and wait to die. After this—starvation."

The prophet considered the woman carefully. Her malnourished face framed frightened eyes, and when she spoke, her lips barely moved, each word escaping her mouth with great effort. The famine in Zarephath was raging, ready to claim this young widow as one of its earliest victims. Why should she show him hospitality even if she had plenty? She was a Gentile, a sorely pressed and frightened one at that. Why should she share her last meal with a vagabond old Jew about whom she knew nothing?

Still, a test is hardly a test if it is easy. Prophets, he mused, know whom to test, and they are shown the nature of the test, but God does not reveal whether those being tested will pass. In fact, he reckoned that lately God seemed less inclined to share more than fragments, mere potsherds of prophetic revelation. He wondered if God was becoming more cantankerous.

Furthermore, why was a prophet never allowed to simply explain the matter? Oh, just to say to the woman, "I am a prophet, you see, and God will miraculously sustain you if you will sustain me. I promise you that if you will share your little with me, God will bestow much on you." Why not just tell her that? No, no, God would never allow that. He likes everybody in the dark. Oh, well—a test is a test.

"Go in the house," he told her. "Make the falafel, and give me some, too." He could not think of how to make it sound less demanding and insensitive. Anyway, he doubted if God would have allowed it. "That's right," he groused at God, "don't make it easy for her."

THE BLINDING LIGHT OF PROMISES

When the widow of Zarephath shared her last meal with the prophet of God, she unleashed the power of giving. The power, the mysterious, miraculous power of giving is so at the heart of who God is that in the giving of His Son, God revealed His very character. When we enter into the sacrament of giving, especially absent the *quid pro quo* that usually dominates our thinking and motives, we release the power of God's character into the atmosphere. Breathable, touching us, and all around us inside and out, the power of giving becomes an unseen grace transforming the moment.

Attempts to turn that principle into an arm's-length business deal with heaven do little but muddy the mystery. Giving and receiving, the wonder of God's dependability, cobbled into a cash-on-the-barrelhead contract, becomes an ugly, self-serving, pedestrian doctrine devoid of true joy and liberty.

Give, and it shall be given unto you...

Yes, yes, yes. A thousand times yes, but become pedantic, demanding, and even cocky about it, and you dilute the wild miracle of it all. Do so, and find only a cold contract where there should have been a sweet romance. Those rigid, self-serving engineers who major in the mechanics of "give to get" would replace the breathtaking risk of covenantal commitment with a bevy of lawyers and a carefully worded prenuptial agreement.

In the first church I pastored, an elderly woman "gave" the church a much-needed organ. It was an act of generosity at which we all rejoiced for a while. We soon realized, however, that the hidden caveat made her "gift" no gift at all. She kept the key at her house!

With no duplicate key allowed, each wedding, rehearsal, funeral, or worship service waited for her to arrive and unlock. That woman and her infernal key dominated every event and soon created such an ocean of ill will that we returned the organ. When she steadfastly refused to surrender the key, we loaded the organ onto a truck and took it to her house.

"What are you doing?" she demanded, as we set it on her front porch.

"Returning your organ."

"But I gave it to the church."

"No," I explained. "No, you didn't. You loaned it, and such an arrangement has become unmanageable. Whoever owns the key owns the organ."

She took her key and her organ to another church in town where it stayed for a while before they also rejected the arrangement. For years afterward, it sat unplayed in her living room, for she knew not a note of music. After her death, the niece to whom it had been willed came to claim the thing. It had to be broken into, for she had hidden the key. To this day I believe she managed, somehow, to have it with her in the coffin. Even from beyond the grave, her "gift" was an act of control and manipulation. Hers was not the beautiful power of giving, but the nastiest kind of power the flesh and the devil possess.

To give openly, joyfully, confident of who God is, but not constantly checking the mailbox, is the power of the miraculous. The financial promises of God are real. Tithing has wonderfully blessed my life, and giving beyond the tithe has opened wellsprings of abundance to me beyond my wildest expectations. I believe in Malachi 3:10:

> Bring ye all the tithes into the storehouse, that there may be meat in mine house, and prove me now herewith, saith the Lord of hosts, if I will not open you the windows of heaven, and pour you out a blessing, that there shall not be room enough to receive it.

Yet all such promises are very like the sun. It will give you light, but if you stare straight at it to make sure it's still shining, you will go blind.

THE POWER OF RECKLESS GIVING

A wild, sweet abandon swept through her, driving before it all care for the eyes of others, all concern for appearances or pride or possessions. No one, nothing mattered except seeing Him, touching Him, showing Him that He and He alone was all of life to her. Let them gape. Let them wonder and raise their brows and think that they knew what they did not. He and He alone was her everything. She wanted only to give without caution, without measurement, holding back nothing, and expecting nothing.

She had experienced so much in so many ways that her jaded soul had become calloused to the touch of others. For money often, sometimes for affection, or even for control she had given only to get. Her inner self unsurrendered, surface to surface, flesh to flesh, even in passion, no man, no moment of lust had ever caused her the faintest impulse to give more than pleasure, at least until now.

Mindless of all others in the room, she hurled herself at His feet. In every fiber of her being there vibrated a profound will to give, no, to surrender, not something, but her all, her everything, her very self. Raising the alabaster box above her head she smashed it on the terrazzo, releasing the pungent aroma of the ointment within. Not counting the cost, oblivious to the opinions of others, in reckless abandon she gave, not to get, but to worship, and in that moment she received more than she gave, the approbation and mercy of Messiah.

"Thy sins are forgiven. Thy faith hath saved thee; go in peace."

The shards of the beautiful box forgotten on the floor behind her, she left not simply that room but her past as well. The expensive ointment was gone, used up, extravagantly wasted in a gesture of love. The alabaster, the most expensive thing owned, could never be repaired. None of what she had given was on her mind, only what she had received. Power, pure, holy power raced through her veins like fire.

THE POWER OF SUBMISSION

Dragged from his cell in the middle of the night and prodded at spear-point through the torch-lit corridors, Barabbas was certain that death awaited him. Ever since his capture the only real question had been when, not whether. He had cut the throat of a Roman sergeant, and the Romans were not a merciful race. Crucifixion was to be his horrible end. No lawyer, no trial, no voice in his defense, just Roman justice, so called, and a Roman death would be the last of Barabbas. He trembled at the thought.

Let it be so. He had given his answer to Rome in blood. "Hades awaits," one of his guards had said. Perhaps, but he had dispatched that fat pig of a Roman sergeant to get there first. He may die on the cross but not as a coward or a collaborator. Barabbas had wet his blade in Roman blood. He feared the cross, feared it beyond words, dreaded it with all the agony of his mind, but at least he had struck a blow first. Rome had the power to kill him now, but he had taught one Roman about the power of a Jew.

"Come on," snarled the guard.

"Why now? Am I to be crucified in the middle of the night?"

"That remains to be seen, Jew. Either you or your king. The governor says the people will decide. Personally, I couldn't care less."

None of this made any sense at all to Barabbas. What king? Let the people decide? Decide what? Still, for a murderer already sentenced to be crucified, any ray of hope was not to be argued with.

Thrust suddenly through the doorway and out onto the elevated portico overlooking the paved courtyard, Barabbas was dumbfounded at what greeted his eyes. The Gabbatha, the paved outer court, was filled with a surly mob seething restlessly in the flickering torchlight. In the middle of the portico stood the governor himself with only an honor guard. On the other end of the porch from Barabbas stood a single man, a tortured bloody remnant of a man so horrifyingly disfigured that an involuntary shiver racked Barabbas. What had they done to His head? These Romans were savages.

"Behold, the man."

The governor, in his aristocratic Latin, thundered the words at the mob. *That,* Barabbas thought, *that is the voice of power.* The response, however, was an immediate crescendo without prelude, a roar of animalistic fury. The shriek of the mob rolled up toward the columned portico, then engulfed the Roman governor and Barabbas in a foaming wave of anger.

"Crucify Him!"

"Away with Him!"

"He is not fit to live."

"Give us Barabbas."

The vile, unrestrained hatred of the mob electrified the air. The power, the stone-breaking, hammering power of their unified disdain was amazing to Barabbas. He saw the governor's eyes and knew the mob would get what they wanted—and what they wanted was Barabbas alive and that poor wretch there crucified. The power of a governor, of an empire really, was overwhelmed by the power of hate. The only one with no power, no hope of power or anything else except a disgusting and lingering death, was that man. He for whose blood they howled like beasts stood unmoving and unmoved by both the mob and the governor.

Barabbas studied Him whom the mob had rejected. That was the truth actually. Barabbas could see that. It was not so much that they had chosen Barabbas, but they had rejected this poor creature, whoever He was.

Power, Barabbas thought, *is what this eerie, torch-lit scene was all about.* Caesar's power, the governor's, the mob's, and the pathetic shred of his own violent strength comingled in a confluence of hate and fear and murder.

The only one with less power than Barabbas, with no power whatsoever, not even to free his own hands, was that man whose death they demanded. Barabbas wondered. What was His name? He doubted if he, or anyone else, would ever know it or remember it. In this world only one thing really mattered—power. The powerful get remembered. The powerless get crucified.

FROM GOOFY TO GLORY

Given the level of misapprehension and downright goofy teachings on the biblical concept of "submission," it is hardly any wonder that few topics energize such rancor and resistance. At the heart of the apostle Paul's letter to the church at Ephesus is a core of pragmatic admonitions to live in the power of submission. The tensions between employers and employees, between husbands and wives, and between parents and children, Paul said, can be overcome by the mystery power of submission.

Many have fastened their gaze only on that single verse that calls upon wives to submit to their husbands (Eph. 5:22). Any text without its context easily becomes the slave of the private agendas of manipulators and narrow-gauge ideologues. A text like Ephesians 5:22, one that calls on wives to be submissive, could be used as a crowbar to leverage women into a subservient role, especially by males with more concern for control than faith in the power of giving.

For such "owners" of verse 22, the problem is verse 21: "Submitting yourselves one to another in the fear of God."

Paul's concept of submission would not create doormat Stepford wives married to domineering husbands, but rather covenant partners in mutual submission. "Submitting to one another" is the foundational truth on which Paul constructed his thesis on relational power. In marriage, in the marketplace, and between parent and child, power derives not from position or physical strength but from submission.

Too much talk of submitted wives and too little understanding of true mutual submission have done much to embitter women and steal from men the power of true submission. The overbearing bore, thumping on his chest and selfishly demanding that his wife and children submit because he's the "head of the household," is more like King Kong than King

Jesus. Jesus is also the head of His household, but not because He ascended to the pinnacle of the temple shouting, "Down, you dogs, and worship Me, or I'll melt you like wax." It was on the cross, giving His life for His bride, crucified to Himself, that the power of Jesus was truly glorified. He died that she might live, became poor that she might become rich, and became sin that she might become the righteousness of God. In attempting to fulfill their biblical mandate, heads of households would do well to remember that. So would CEOs, and college presidents and pastors. Leading is about submission, and submission is about giving.

SUBMISSION AS REBELLION

Imagine that a wife and husband have an argument over breakfast. That's not too hard to imagine. He leaves for work at a local car repair shop, and five minutes away from home he has forgotten the argument. Males have no memory for the retention of arguments. It is God's little joke on women, who, on the other hand, have such a memory.

All day she rehearses the argument, remembering every syllable of every mean thing he said and the nasty way his lip curled as he said it. That afternoon when he happily throws wide the door to his castle, he is utterly oblivious to the firestorm waiting inside. He only knows he has had a horrible day at work, he is home, and the bride of his youth is waiting inside.

"I'm home, Baby," he cries at first sight of her. "Give me a kiss."

Fixing him with a stony gaze she thinks to herself, *Not on his best day.* Having attended a dozen Christian marriage seminars, however, she has learned one thing: "Wives, submit yourselves unto your husbands." That much she knows.

"Fine," she snaps at him. "You want a kiss? Fine. I'll give you a kiss because I want you to know who the Christian in this marriage is. The Bible says wives should submit to their husbands, so here's your kiss, in the name of Jesus." With that she pecks him on the cheek with all the warmth and affection of a nail gun.

That is not submission. That is rebellion, cold, angry rebellion. It is a manipulative ploy in the name of Jesus, a play for power, for dominance in her own home, one designed to intimidate and put her husband on the defensive. Worst of all, she actually believes she has submitted.

When believers yield to His will, God does not want begrudging, reluctant laborers, but happy warriors, joyful just to be called upon. He wants us to receive His will as our own, to enter into it as though we had thought of it ourselves.

THE POWER OF JESUS' MIND

Submission is giving, and the power of giving is at the very heart of who God is. To express His eternal, unalloyed Fatherliness, God gave His Son. To express His submission to the will of the Father, the Son gave His life. The Father's gift met by the submission of the Son meant power, a power infinitely beyond the world's and all its kingdoms and armies.

> Let this mind be in you, which was also in Christ *Jesus*: who, being in the form of God, thought it not robbery to be equal with God: but *made himself of no reputation,* and *took upon him the form of a servant,* and was made in the likeness of men: and being found in fashion as a man, he *humbled himself,* and *became obedient unto death, even the death of the cross.*
> —PHILIPPIANS 2:5–8,
> EMPHASIS ADDED

To understand the mind of Christ and the essence of His power, read the *italicized* words as a single sentence: *Jesus made Himself of no reputation, became a servant, humbled Himself, and became obedient unto the death of the cross.*

The church has majored in denouncing worldliness but has seldom understood what it is—at least, not at a level any more profound than clothesline holiness. Worldliness is nothing other than trusting and operating in systems of power contrary to that mind that was in Christ.

◆ Jesus' mind despised image for what it was. The worldly mind cares for little else.

◆ Jesus' mind found power in servant leadership. The worldly mind demands dominion and preeminence.

◆ Jesus' mind held humility to be the key to power. The worldly mind clings desperately to its pride.

◆ Jesus' mind was obedient. The worldly mind is full of rebellion.

◆ Jesus' mind embraced the cross that others might live. The worldly mind clutches at survival, even if others must die.

Worldliness in its most nefarious form is not about makeup and short skirts. It is about church boards that plot coups and energize gossipy phone campaigns and indulge rebellion. Worldliness is not in what is worn but in the way the mind works. Worldliness, above all things, says, "God will not take care of this, at least not the way I want, so I must do it." Worldliness is, in the final analysis, any denial of the sovereignty and power of God.

The mind of Christ, that humble, obedient mind, that mind that embraced the power of the cross, is the mind that trusts God even in death. The worldly mind is the mind of control, manipulation, rebellion, and, finally, witchcraft. The worldly mind seizes the reins from God Himself and, once in control, demands its own way and serves its own will.

Ultimately, of course, the power of the world is short-lived. He who comes by the gun is overcome by the gun. Church bureaucracies, when riddled by Byzantine intrigue and ruled over by the ruthless politicians, lose that mind that was in Christ—and all spiritual power.

Those who choose the politics of power will have only the power of politics. When, in humble grace, in the spirit of servant leadership, in sacrificial, giving submission they seek the mind of Christ, He will grant them His power.

THE POWER OF INFLUENCE

The king's passion could not explain it, for as lovely as she was, the world, his world, was full of beautiful women. Love, whatever kind of love could live in the heart of a man like Xerxes, might make even a king listen to a mere woman, but Xerxes, if he loved her, had never said so. It was not his way.

Chosen, wed, added to the king's harem, and called for only when he wanted her for a night or an hour, Esther was a "queen" with no power. If, as she was constantly being told, every young girl in Persia envied her, it was only because they knew nothing of her real life. With a palace for a prison and a husband whom she dared not approach without being summoned, she was lonely and fearful and friendless. Except for her uncle Mordecai, the only Jew in the entire palace complex, she was despised by the other women for her place as queen, a place she would gladly have traded to any barefoot shepherdess.

Now, with her life and the lives of her people hanging by the slender thread of her ability to touch and turn the heart of a tyrant not known for his mercy, Esther could not fully explain what had happened. The king wanted her, but not, she thought, enough to execute his senior most adviser. Xerxes had effectively reversed his own policy, an unprecedented action in an empire where the word of the emperor was divine, irreversible law. Because her eyes were big and brown? Because of a dinner party? She thought not.

At first when her uncle Mordecai had informed her of the plot by Haman to exterminate the Jews and seize their properties, she had hoped to remain above the fray. This was ludicrous, of course, since, sooner or later, her own Jewish bloodline would have become known. This Mordecai had pointed out to her in no uncertain terms. Not truly a coward, Esther had simply seen herself as powerless to help. If she even entered Xerxes' presence without being bidden she could be killed. Beyond that, even if she did live to make her appeal, why would Xerxes listen?

Now that it was over, she could hardly believe it herself. Haman was hanged on his own gallows, her beloved uncle was promoted and honored by the king, and her people were saved from a horrifying genocide. What mysterious power had worked in the heart of the king to cause such a miraculous deliverance?

She who hadn't even a dagger had dissuaded him whose armies were a vast host. A young woman, a girl really, without real authority, without political allies, incredibly naïve in matters of palace intrigue, had caused a pagan warrior-king to turn aside from a bloodthirsty plan that would have enriched him immeasurably. Xerxes had every reason to execute the treacherous plan of Haman and no logical reason to abort it. Yet it was Haman whom he executed, only Persians who were killed, and the condemned Jews escaped alive. Furthermore, a trusted adviser of Xerxes' own race was hanged and replaced with a Jew.

What mysterious power had there been in the meal she served the king? Nothing she had added. No, something else, something more than sexual attraction and a well-fed monarch had wrought this miracle. God? Surely. Esther knew that the God of Abraham had undertaken for His people in Persia.

What mystery of God had she tapped into, that a powerless Jewess could be used in so great a way to change the mind of so great a man in so terrible a moment? Having no name to call it, Esther, the Jewish wife of her Gentile overlord, shrugged her girlish shoulders and prayed never to need it, whatever *it* was, ever again.

GOD IN A GODLESS BOOK

Perhaps the most astonishing paradox in the Bible is that, in the only book in the Old or New Covenants *not* to mention God, God moves mightily to save a nation. Rosh Hashanah, the Festival of Lights, commemorates the miraculous story of Esther's victory over Haman, and, for that matter, over the emperor Xerxes.

Some writers, both religious and secular, have attempted to make this precious story out to be a story of secular humanism, a glorification of man's (or more precisely, woman's) wisdom. Religious commentators have sometimes despised the Book of Esther for not actually *saying* God, while secularists have erroneously claimed it as their toehold in the Bible, a history book without reference to the Lord of history.

Both are pathetically mistaken. Frequently the most authentic spirituality makes the most sparing reference to God. The Book of Esther assumes that the God of wisdom grants Mordecai wisdom, that the God of the Jews undertakes to spare them, and that only a young girl's faith in her God could fill her with such boldness. There is little need to point out the obvious.

This truth may actually make the case for Esther to be ranked among the most spiritually mature books in the Bible. When people of faith and courage trapped in an alien culture act in accordance with God's will, He is alive in the process, present in the people, and glorified in the outcome. As believers seek to magnify the Lord in the postmodern, post-Christian, post-almost-everything-holy-and-godly era, Esther is just the hero they need.

To assume that a holy and miraculous God is not moving in and through every moment of Esther's story just because He is not mentioned is nearly as silly as denying the presence of Satan in the book just because he isn't mentioned. The mind behind the mind of Haman, the same anti-Semitic mind behind

Pharaoh and Hitler and Stalin, is, likewise on every page. An elderly rabbi once told me that when one looked at the holocaust, he could see how someone might deny the reality of God, but how, he marveled, could anyone doubt the reality of Satan?

Whether in Auschwitz in 1943 or in Susa in 473 B.C., the ongoing war of the worlds, power against power, is the underlying reality of human history. World War II was not about the division of Europe. It was about the creation of Israel. As satanic spirits urged Nazi guards on to the slaughter before them, it is quite probable that neither guard nor demon nor many of the victims realized that God was moving in history to regather the children of Abraham to the Land. Likewise, we probably have little or no idea what God is about in this godless age in which we now live and lead. Esther is the very book for us postmoderns, and hers is the power we need.

THE DIVINE RECIPE

There is a television cook who delights me no end, not with his recipes, about which I know nothing and care little, but with his performance. He is manly, exuberant, and full of joy as he hurls, literally hurls ingredients at his TV stove. Blasting some under-construction pasta dish with bits of exotic mushrooms, then pitching in diced pimientos, and, at last, lashing the whole thing with herbs like fast balls, he always shouts the same thing. *Bam!* I love it. A combination of Batman and Martha Stewart yelping *bam* while recklessly tossing recipes together with a style more like a sumo wrestler's than a chef's. *Bam!*

I often think if only I were in some certain position, if only I were president or governor or whatever, then I would have power to change things. The fact of the matter is, those who hold those positions frequently feel utterly powerless in them.

Pu Yi, at the death of the Dowager Empress, became the infant emperor of China, lord of all he surveyed, ruler of the masses, and a pathetic prisoner. First, as a child he was imprisoned in the Forbidden City, controlled by the army of eunuchs who administered the ancient capital. Later he was driven out of the Forbidden City by the revolutionary guard during WWII, only to become a prisoner of lust and fashion, a laughable playboy, mocked behind his back by the Europeans and Americans he imitated. Then, deceived and dominated by the Japanese invaders, he was made an "emperor," a hollow title, of the puppet state of Manchukuo, or Manchuria. At the end of his life, he died a prisoner of the Communists, an humble gardner in a drab grey uniform.

The last emperor of China was not the only ruler to feel imprisoned by his position. We think of such persons holding power, and certainly there is truth to that, but, in many ways, power holds them.

Xerxes, considered a god by his empire, was himself a prisoner of his own power. Because he was a god, his word was divine law. It could not be reversed. Even when he learned the truth about Haman's plot and his faithful Jewish subjects, though he longed to change his mind, he could not. More than one proud, egotistical, positional leader, trapped by the immutability of his word, has been totally unable to admit error, reverse a decision, or change his mind. What a terrible prison.

The only two people in the Book of Esther with true power, the power to foil a deadly plot, get an evil adviser executed, and turn the heart of Xerxes, the only two with that kind of power were Mordecai and Esther.

They accomplished what not even Xerxes could do: alter the outcome decreed by a Persian god-king powerless to change his own mind. Haman, dangling from a rope on the very gallows he had built for Mordecai, was the proof that there is a mysterious recipe of power that transcends position. Without true power kings are slaves, and with it slaves may move the hearts of kings. That power is the power of influence.

The recipe includes divine opportunity made possible by the hand of God combined with the blessing of biblical favor and mixed with just the right amount of godly wisdom and Spirit-led timing. The result is the power of influence. This unassuming, often faceless power is actually quite explosive. *Bam!*

Wise leaders, presidents, principals, and kings alike surround themselves with wise counselors. The best CEOs know that they are only as good as the advisors around them. Those who counsel the king have roles of great responsibility because of their level of access. At the dark heart of the Nixonian era was a paranoid president surrounded by unprincipled advisers who turned the oval office into a den of thieves. Clinton's catastrophe might have been different entirely had someone influenced him away from his course of survival at any cost. One wonders if any person of influence ever once said, "Mr. President, come clean with America, and lead us out of this nightmare. Even if it costs you the presidency, the national conscience is of greater importance than your reelection."

Both Nixon and Clinton, each in his own way, became, at the end of their presidencies, hollow men dominated and directed by conscienceless handlers. Poor Pu Yi, the emperor of China, ruled over by palace eunuchs, never had any real power. The power, for good or evil, often lies not with the king but with his council.

EARNED INFLUENCE

In the Book of Esther, influence was wielded by an elderly Jewish bureaucrat and a long-ignored wife lost in an oriental harem. In Nehemiah, a lowly cupbearer influenced a great king to release the Jews from bondage and to allow Jerusalem to be rebuilt. The Gentile Ruth influenced her bitter Jewish mother-in-law to trust God and dream again. Daniel, a slave, so profoundly influenced Nebuchadnezzar that when the emperor's grandson needed wisdom, discernment, and interpretation, the elderly Daniel was called out of retirement.

Throughout the Bible, wives, sons, daughters, and slaves influenced leaders for God and for good. Before the divine opportunity is granted, the power of influence must be earned. Esther, Mordecai, Ruth, and Daniel all proved their loyalty and devotion to duty long before the opportunity for influence arose. Access for influence is earned by a proven track record. Influence is gained by those who do well at what is given them. Influence in crisis is a factor of trust earned over time.

Furthermore, the true power of godly influence must be used both sparingly and unselfishly. Esther and Mordecai left the crass manipulation to Haman. Haman wanted position, prominence, and prosperity. He controlled Xerxes with carefully edited information about the Jews. Leadership is always at the mercy of the information it receives. Those who, like Haman, have a track record of filtered data and manipulative control will have only limited influence in a crisis and may lose everything. Better a faithful slave or a loyal cupbearer than an unprincipled palace courtier.

THE SELFLESS POWER

Ronald Reagan once said, "There is no limit to what can be accomplished if no one cares who gets the credit." Likewise, the power of influence is virtually inexhaustible so long as it remains silent. In the Book of Esther, three people at one time or another find favor in Xerxes' eyes and influence his decision. At the end of the story, one is beloved, one is promoted, and one is executed. The only one executed was he who squandered his influence on self-promotion.

If God has given you favor in a leader's eyes, wait, I say, wait on the Lord. Use your influence sparingly, unselfishly, and silently. Do not make much with others of your influence upon his leadership. Envy is a terrible and deadly force. Then when leadership, due in part to your influence, makes the right decision, deny that you had anything to do with it. Wise influencers will let the president be noble, the king be merciful, and the owner prove shrewd in business.

Influence that takes the credit may well get a cold shoulder in the next crisis. Herod's wife and stepdaughter used all their influence in a sexually charged, highly public way. They got what they wanted, John the Baptist's head on a platter, but they are never mentioned again. Joshua, on the other hand, who never insinuated himself into Moses' office, was his favored adviser and deputy for forty years and became his anointed successor.

THE POWER OF DOWNWARD INFLUENCE

Unfortunately, many leaders, even those who are aware of the influence being exerted upon them, fail to recognize the power of their own influence upon others. Even more often they fritter away their influence in petty little power games. I once visited a pastor who had sawed the legs off the visitor's chair in his study. He said that intimidated those who sat there, made them feel small, peering over the edge of the desk like insignificant children. This same man told me that when he met a business leader for lunch, he was always a bit late. His reasoning was that the less important person always waits for the greater. What folly! What prideful, manipulative, silly games! Is it any wonder that later some of those businessmen over which he had towered and whom he had made to wait voted him out in a major church revolt.

Jesus cared more for His influence upon the few closest at hand than for His image among the masses. The life of the leader, his character, and his servant spirit will do much to influence his closest associates.

Here is the rule. The closer to the area of immediate impact, the greater the influence. A preacher may, even from so great a distance, have some small influence upon the bloke in the back row. His long-time associate, his secretary, and his kids know the real man, and upon their lives and souls he writes the story of his own character.

I heard someone recently deriding poor Monica Lewinsky. They said, and I quote, "She is nothing but an empty shell looking for some place to perform, and nobody cares anymore." That, sadly, may even be the truth. The tragedy, of course, is that whatever she is may be the result of the influence of others upon her life. I think of a young woman, highly impressionable, in the most powerful room in the world, with the most powerful man in the world. What might he have helped her to become? If she is nothing more than a sick joke on late-night TV, she is not her own creation entirely. She is, like all the intimate followers of leaders everywhere, the workmanship of his deepest influence.

THE POWER OF CHRIST'S INFLUENCE

After the cross, after all their betrayals and denials and disappointments, the apostles became what they became in great part because of the influence of Jesus. As they walked in wisdom and grew in grace, surely, upon occasion, they saw Christ in each other. In the way one or the other would turn a phrase while preaching or pray aloud or even work a miracle, the others would surely smile at each other knowingly: "That looked just like Jesus." "Your voice just then reminded me so of Him." "That is exactly the way He used to do it."

What they were, the giants they became, how they lived, and how they died were reflections of Jesus' power. His influence upon them as well as His spirit within them was the power by which they turned the world upside down.

Not one of the apostles was ever a king or a prince or a president. None ever held any office or ruled a country or ran a company. Yet they lived their lives in power, His power. They served and gave and submitted themselves to God and humanity even as they had seen Him do. Theirs was never the power of the present age, but the timeless, mysterious, eternal power of the suffering servant.

When they died—some by the sword, some in the fire, and one on a cross—they were not powerless victims. They were more than conquerors.